Transactions 2

WHY STUDY ITALIAN

DIVERSE PERSPECTIVES ON A THEME

Edited by

Roberto Dolci
&
Anthony Julian Tamburri

CALANDRA INSTITUTE TRANSACTIONS

CALANDRA INSTITUTE TRANSACTIONS is a series dedicated to studies and analyses that are longer than the usual journal article and shorter than the usual monograph. It will publish manuscripts that fall within these parameters and that deal with any aspect of Italian Americana.

Library of Congress Control Number: 2012924067

CALANDRA INSTITUTE TRANSACTIONS
VOLUME 2

ISBN 978-1-939323-01-9

©2013 by the Authors and the
John D. Calandra Italian American Institute

published by
John D. Calandra Italian American Institute
Queens College/CUNY
25 West 43rd Street, 17th Floor
New York, NY 10038
www.qc.calandra.edu

Table of Contents

"Preface"
 Roberto Dolci & Anthony Julian Tamburri (1)

"Introduction"
 Hon. Giulio Terzi di Sant'Agata (5)

"Why Study Italian" (7)
 Hon. Natalia Quintavalle

"Italian and The Hispanic World in The United States: Latinos in Trans-historical Perspective"
 Clorinda Donato (9)

"Studying Italian: A Linguistic Perspective"
 Hermann W. Haller (17)

"Why I Studied Italian"
 Fred Gardaphé (23)

"Italian as A Consumer Good"
 Silvana Mangione (29)

"Consuming in Italian: Nourishment of the Mind"
 Lidia Bastianich (33)

"Why Study Italian?"
 Vincenzo Marra (35)

"Prima cominci, meglio è": The sooner you start, the better"
 Berardo Paradiso (39)

"Fashion and Translation: The Global Language of Italian Style"
 Eugenia Paulicelli (43)

"Study Abroad in Italy"
 Roberto Dolci (51)

"Learning from the Medicis: Patronage at Work" (63)
 Anthony Julian Tamburri

"Italian: A Gateway to Europe, A Bridge to the Future" (73)
 Hon. Claudio Bisogniero

Contributors (77)

Index of Names (83)

Acknowledgments

We are grateful to the various contributors of this collection, who made a special effort to take time away from their regular duties and activities in order to participate in this project. We also wish to thank members of the Italy's Embassy to the United States in Washington, D.C.: Giulio Terzi di Sant'Agata, Minister for Foreign Affairs, former Ambassador to the United States; Cristiano Maggipinto, Minister Plenipotentiary; and Lucia Dalla Montà, Director of the Education Office.

We also thank Clorinda Donato for her keen editorial suggestions and Lisa Cicchetti for supervising the design of the book's cover.

Preface

The idea for this editorial project was born out of discussions that paralleled those that were taking place around the re-implementation of the Advanced Placement Program in Italian, which the College Board had suspended after the 2010 administration of the Advanced Placement Exam in Italian.

The goal, therefore, of this collection is not to speak to the specifics of the Advanced Placement Program in Italian in any direct way. Instead, we sought to gather an array of different voices that could speak to the general question, "Why study Italian," which we present here in its somewhat ambiguous manner. The phrase, "Why study Italian," may indeed be understood as either a statement or an interrogative. The underlying issue, to be sure, is that Italian is, today, a language very much alive, useful, and employed by many in an array of venues and sectors across the world.

The numbers on Italian and who speaks and studies it are readily available. Within the United States, for example, we have seen the rise in number of who speaks Italian through a variety of venues. The Modern Language Association has tracked college enrollments in Italian since 1969; the increase since that year has been incredible, having multiplied seven times over. The number of students surveyed by the American Council on the Teaching of Foreign Languages (ACTFL), who enroll in Italian in grades K-12, is equally impressive, here too increasing exponentially from year to year.

Further still, with regard to who speaks Italian and where in the United States, for example, one need only consult the 2009 study by Drs. Vincenzo Milione and Christine Gambino, *Sì, Parliamo Italiano! Globalization of the Italian Culture in the United States*.[1] This study constituted a first of a kind when it appeared; it examined how we might arrive at a more accurate number of people who actually speak Italian in the United States. In so doing, the authors looked at the social surveys available to the public and analyzed those figures against the background of a century-long evolution of

---

[1] Vincenzo Milione and Christine Gambino, *Sì, Parliamo Italiano! Globalization of the Italian Culture in the United States* (New York: Calandra Institute, 2009).

the speaking, studying, and teaching of Italian nation-wide. What the reader of this study ultimately comes to understand is that the socio-linguistic landscape for Italian is actually much more broad than one might have thought, precisely because the current tools available to us are, simply stated, out-dated and, to some degree, dismissive willy-nilly of the situation.

Some of the results from *Sì, Parliamo Italiano* demonstrate that (1) the number of people reported to speak the language is significantly underestimated, and (2) the range of people who actually speak the language is, historically speaking, limited in scope, since the social surveys such as the Census have always asked *de facto* qualificatory questions with tags such as what language is spoken "at home" or if it is the "primary" language spoken. As the authors demonstrated, such questions can only restrict the numerical results, thus ignoring those instead who, for other reasons still, speak the language on a daily basis either at work or in other situations that do not fall within the boundaries of the strictly familiar or personal.

Proof of the *necessity* of Italian as a *practical*, quotidian language was, to be sure, emphatically underscored by New York City's Mayor Michael R. Bloomberg's Executive Order 120 (22 July 2008). The order requires all city agencies to provide translation assistance to those linguistically dependent on the top six languages spoken by New Yorkers, which include: Spanish, Chinese, Russian, Korean, Italian, and French Creole. In guaranteeing access to programs, services, and activities for our limited-English-proficient sisters and brothers, there is a new Customer Service Group housed in the Mayor's Office of Operations, which works in concert with the Mayors Office of Immigrant Affairs in order to assist in the application of Executive Order 120. In October 2011, a similar executive order was passed at the state level: "Based on census data, the services will be offered in Spanish, Chinese, Italian, Russian, French, and French Créole." The announcement of the Executive Order went on to state: "Approximately two and a half million New Yorkers do not speak English as their primary language and have limited ability to read, speak, write, or understand English. This presents potential barriers when trying to access important government benefits or services."[2]

---

[2] For more detailed information about Governor Andrew M. Cuomo's Executive Order, see the following website: http://www.governor.ny.gov/press/10062011nonenglisheo.

What both Executive Orders also speak to, as well, is both the necessity and, we underscore, the value, of language(s) other than English as daily vehicles for communication.

As others have pointed out in the past, and as some of our colleagues underscore herein, in both an implicit and explicit manner, Italian is a language that has been and continues to be a significant mode of communication from a plethora of reasons valid still today: it is the communicative vehicle of one of the West's most influential cultures since the 1200s; it remains an effective language of daily communication beyond the geo-confines of Italy; it is a language of finance and commerce. These are just some of the reasons why Italian remains an important language with/through which we still communicate an array of messages and communiqués. Precisely because of these reasons Italian figures as its own sort of lingua franca, on the one hand. In a similar fashion, on the other hand, we can also consider Italian, in the broadest sense of the term, as a most practical language that allows us access to a variety of worlds that subtend an internationalization of peoples from all aspects imaginable.

Roberto Dolci & Anthony Julian Tamburri
PERUGIA–NEW YORK, SPRING–FALL, 2012

Introduction

Giulio Terzi di Sant'Agata
Minister of Foreign Affairs, Italy

The Italian language is increasingly appreciated in the United States. According to the most recent Modern Language Association Survey, the number of Italian students in American universities has increased by almost 60% since 1998, thus jumping from 49,000 to 80,752. According to other sources, Italian is the only European language whose elective study is on the rise in the United States, both on a high school and on a university level. Italy is the second most requested destination for studying abroad. Every year an average of more than 25,000 American students (there were 30,361 in 2011) pursue Italian language, culture and art studies at Italian universities and on the Italian campuses of American universities.

In New York, on November 10, 2010 the President of the College Board announced the reinstatement of Italian in the AP Program. I consider this as a key achievement for the promotion and diffusion of Italian language in the United States. This is a success for the Italian government, for the Italian people who love our language and will benefit from its growing presence, for the Italian-American community who was such a staunch supporter of this endeavor, and for Italian corporations who believed in, and backed, this project since the campaign's inception. Italian language played, plays and will continue to play an extraordinary role in the development of human society, economy and culture.

The role of which I am speaking is that of Dante's language in literature; of Gaetano Filangieri's mother tongue in his correspondence with Benjamin Franklin on the U.S. Constitution; the language of Federico Fellini, Roberto Rossellini and Pier Paolo Pasolini in modern cinematography; the expression of Valentino and Armani in fashion. Or again, the words of science and technology voiced by Antonio Meucci, by Enrico Fermi and the many physicists who to this day work at the FermiLab in Illinois, or yet of inventor Guglielmo Marconi, whom a unique bilingual and bi-curricular school is named after in New York. And talking of schools and education, let me recall that this book is also dedicated to teachers, so of course I must mention the

Italian of Maria Montessori, whose methodology inspired thousands of schools internationally, particularly in the United States.

The Italian language has always been the driving force behind our culture: indeed, Italy as a cultural and linguistic entity precedes its political unification by some six centuries. The Italian language, therefore, has also played a pivotal role in the 150th anniversary of Italy's unification which we celebrated throughout the United States, and is even more critical at this time, as we celebrate 2013, year of Italian culture in the United States, with programs touching upon all aspects of Italian cultural heritage – from cinema, to art, music and literature – as well as Italy's talent in joining tradition with innovation and scientific and technological research.

Italian is also a language which binds Europe and the United States on an even deeper level: the political thought which gave birth, over two and a half centuries ago, to a lasting and shared idea of democracy is based upon the philosophical and juridical principles elaborated by the eighteenth-century Neapolitan philosopher Gaetano Filangieri, whose writings Benjamin Franklin knew so well and with whom he corresponded so intensely.

Another important thought regarding the study of foreign languages, to include Italian, is that the complexity of today's world makes more than one *lingua franca* a necessity for future generations. The challenge that awaits America and Europe in this millennium is to recognize pluralism and diversity. By improving education through the study of foreign languages we can contribute to the values of peace, solidarity and progress.

In Italy, this pattern is enshrined in the Constitution and has developed considerably in the last sixty years. Italy introduced the teaching of foreign languages, even in primary schools, in the early 1990s. For over ten years now, junior high school students have been learning two foreign languages. The most recent high school reform requires that one subject be taught in a language other than Italian.

New generations deserve to be exposed to real cultural pluralism as much as possible. In this pluralism, the study of Italian is not only essential, given the contributions of Italian culture to our common heritage, but – allow me to say – a particularly enjoyable pursuit.

Why Study Italian

Natalia Quintavalle
Consul General of Italy to New York

We Italians do not have a strong tradition of studying foreign languages, mainly because we are very proud of our own Italian language and thus convinced that no other language is as perfect as ours. We also have a natural easiness in establishing relationships, which makes us very good at exporting goods and services and equally adept at welcoming foreigners without the benefit of a good knowledge of our interlocutor's language.

However, what a difference there is when we are able to talk with the relative confidence of being understood, without using those exaggerated hand gestures with the lingering risk of being completely misunderstood!

When I was eleven, upon entering junior high school I was asked to choose between English and French: my parents chose French for me, and later on I also studied English as well as some German and Arabic. As a result, my French is very good, my English is fairly good, and even with my poor German and Arabic I can nonetheless feel at ease in many other countries. Moreover, I feel that the knowledge of different languages makes me able to better understand the psychology of other people, including Italians.

So, why study Italian?

Firstly, to make sure you are understood in Italy, where sooner or later you will certainly travel – for tourism, work, culture or "love," as it frequently happens.

Secondly, to have an inside view of the psychology of your interlocutor, be it your friend, host, client, or your potential future husband or wife.

Thirdly, if you are an Italian American you could comprehend at last what your grandmother wanted to communicate to you when she was saying *"ogni scarrafone e' bello a mamma sua."*

On a different yet equally serious note, the effort of the Italian Government to promote the teaching of the Italian language is truly an important and worthwhile one. Furthermore, it has been vigorously endorsed by numerous Italian-American organizations, underscoring a genuine, productive collaboration between Italy and the Italian-American community

The reinstatement of Italian in the College Board's 2012 Advanced Placement Program is an unmistakable testimony to the increasing interest in our language (as, for instance, Haller underscores herein) and to the commitment of the Ministry of Foreign Affairs. Young and not so young people are increasingly attracted by the possibility of communicating with Italian partners, understanding the librettos of the opera, reading the Italian newspapers, among numerous other reasons one might opt for Italian.

Italian is not an easy language to learn, but it is certainly easier if you already speak Spanish (Donato readily demonstrates as much in her contribution herein), as a large percentage of people in NYC, for instance, already do. And, with regard to all the other languages, the sooner you start studying them, the quicker you become fluent. This is the reason why our current priority is to encourage the teaching of Italian in the primary schools and to support those programs devoted to training teachers of Italian.

Thanks to the attentive work of the Italian Cultural Institute, the Italian American Committee on Education (IACE), La Scuola d'Italia Guglielmo Marconi, and the many teachers of Italian working in American schools and colleges, it is easier today to gain access to our language. Yet, there is always room for improvement, and we are confident that with the help of the Italian American organizations and the American schools colleges and cultural institutions – such as the Calandra Institute, which we acknowledge also for this interesting publication – many more Americans will become enamored of Dante's language.

ITALIAN AND THE HISPANIC WORLD IN THE UNITED STATES
LATINOS IN TRANSHISTORICAL PERSPECTIVE

Clorinda Donato
California State University, Long Beach

Just as the field of translation studies continually reinscribes the relevance of world literature through new renderings capable of transferring and connecting languages, ideas, peoples and cultures over space and time, academic disciplines should likewise continually reassess the when and the where of their activity to ensure relevance to the students they seek to serve. Current humanities research on the creation and function of networks as the primary means of knowledge transfer in the Republic of Letters has much to offer to those of us who ponder the relevance of Italian in the United States today. Indeed, Bruno Latour's *Reassembling the social*, provides definitions and models for understanding the social that are wholly applicable to questions of language study and audience, which is the larger theme of this essay.[1] Latour asks us to focus our attention on the associations through which the social is constituted, as well as its shifting nature through movement of "actors" into spaces where new assemblages are formed; thus the social is precarious and shifting, in need of continual reassessment and reconstitution. Actors and their associations undergo processes of "translation" or metamorphosis, in each mode of reassemblage.[2] This provocative method of approaching the social as no longer a fixed, *a priori* entity, has had deep implications for the social sciences and the humanities in the field of knowledge transfer and those groups or assemblages whose behavior suggests that they would be more inclined to take up a particular set of practices or habits. Let us consider how it might have equally significant implications in the field of language study, pertinent to the topic of this volume, "Why study Italian?"

---

[1] Bruno Latour, *Reassembling the Social: An Introduction to Actor-Network-Theory*, UK: Oxford University Press, 2005.
[2] See Book Reviews: Reassembling the Social, Review 2 by Florian Teufelhart & Wiebke Pohler, University of Munich (LMU), in *Space and Culture*, http://www.spaceandculture.org/2009/03/24/bookreiews-reassembling-the-social.

When we approach the question, "Why study Italian," our first tendency might be to extol the virtues of learning a language of culture, the arts and cuisine, while advocating, as well, for the importance of Italian as a language of historical importance in the immigration history of the United States. We know that students like Italian, and unfortunately, many of these discussions and encouragements fall into the range of Italian as entertainment. Italian is "fun" to learn (pizza, pasta, e Pinocchio) and Italy is a "fun" place to visit. As instructors of Italian, we have incorporated as many functional lessons as we can into our repertoires, focusing ever so many lessons on enticing PowerPoint demonstrations of Italy's finest cuisines and fashions. And while these attributes of Italian language and culture will never cease to attract admirers, many of them students, we often undermine our own discipline by not contemplating other reasons for which students might study Italian, or how changing demographics might influence how we teach, as well as the particular corpus of the Italian curriculum we teach.

Throughout the United States, the college-seeking demographic has changed, most noticeably through rising numbers of Hispanic students, a reality I have first-hand knowledge of at my university. California State University, Long Beach was designated a Hispanic-Serving Institution a number of years ago, when the percentage of the student body that identified as Latino topped 30%. Hispanic-Serving Institutions seek "to expand educational opportunities for, and improve the attainment of, Hispanic students."[3] This demographic continues to rise. When the 2010 census numbers are finalized, it is anticipated that Latinos alone will comprise 17-18 per cent of the U.S. population. Already, in the States of California and Texas, they are 37.6 per cent; when analyzed by age, Latinos under the age of 18 make up more than 50 per cent of the youth population; in 2006 they had a purchasing power of $789 billion, a figure that is expected to reach $1 trillion this year. What are the implications of these shifts for the study of Italian in the United States? Can this demographic movement in any way be correlated with other data, for example, the data that has emerged from ACTFL about language preferences among American high school students? This is where Latour's research can be used to analyze this demographic data in relationship to trends in lan-

---

[3] There are currently 234 Hispanic-Serving Institutions (HSI's) in the United States, for a total of 10% of the Institutions of higher learning in the United States.

guage study in the United States. The executive summary of the American Council on Foreign Language Teaching 2010 Annual Report in the "Key Findings" section states: "Spanish, French, and Italian continue to be the languages most desired by students, while slightly less than 10% of students want to study Japanese, German, and American Sign Language."[4] Students who vote in these ACTFL surveys are not asked to identify their ethnic background, yet this might be a category to add to future surveys, to see how language preference relates to ethnic origin.

Thus, if we apply Latour's method of tracking the movement of the "actors" into and out of assemblages, we immediately notice the surging numbers of Hispanic students who populate American institutions of higher education, a new assemblage whose burgeoning numbers are transforming the dynamics of the language-acquisition classroom. As we analyze who is acting within the sites of higher education in our country and if we pay attention to where the consequences of associations may travel, it is not difficult to find that the language classrooms of Hispanic-Serving Institutions register increasing numbers of Hispanic students. When they get to college, these students "move" in the direction of French, Italian, and Spanish language courses, which may well account for the preference for these languages among Hispanic students and the increased numbers in Italian language programs everywhere.

I would like to contextualize these somewhat speculative comments by continuing with my examination of California State University, Long Beach as a case study. Spanish language and Hispanic culture pervade the California landscape. If you speak Spanish, you have relationships that non-Spanish speakers don't have. As an Italian American, or a speaker of Italian, you may also have relationships of similar intensity, for many Italians also identify as Latino and indeed, a brief Google search reveals that there is an ongoing discussion about the definition of Latino, with a particular focus on the use of the term in relationship to Italians and Italian Americans in the United States. While much of this is anecdotal, the sheer numbers of people who comment or inquire about this topic means that there is serious thinking taking place about the relationships between the peoples, languages, and cultures that might be considered Latino. Indeed, the vast majority of these com-

---

[4] See report at http://www.actfl.org/files/ACTFLReport2010FINAL.pdf.

ments conclude by linking in some way Italians with Latinos and agreeing that the term "Latino" might indeed be shared. In a well-articulated article on the topic, "¿Hispanic or Latino?", Richard Vásquez comments, "I've heard no objections if Italians want to start sharing the phrase."[5] Other sites ask questions such as "How Come Lots of Italians Look Latino?" or "How Come Lots of Latinos Look Italian?"; other sites emphasize parallels in culinary and musical taste, citing the vast numbers of Italian artists whose careers are as flourishing in Spanish as they are in Italian, artists such as Laura Pausini and Eros Ramazzotti. Both artists have spoken enthusiastically about their crossover success, blurring the lines between themselves and their Hispanic fans.[6] And in article after article, Ramazzotti, an Italian, is defined as a "Latin" singer, along with the Puerto Rican, Ricky Martin, and the Spaniard, Enrique Iglesias. In these articles the term "Latin" is used to agglomerate Italian and Hispanic singers under the single ethnic descriptor, "Latin." In the world of music and art, then, this conflation reflects the increasing "rapprochement" of cultures whose artists share enough common cultural and linguistic ground as to be comfortably placed under the same ethnic rubric.

I have been at California State University, Long Beach for twenty-four years. In that time I have noticed that increasing percentages of students in both French and Italian classes have Hispanic first and/or last names. A very high percentage of these students are heritage speakers of Spanish, while nearly all the rest have studied Spanish in high school. Even the non-Latino students come with a background in high school Spanish, which in many cases puts them at a linguistic advantage that parallels the advantage of the heritage speaker. I have paid special attention to how Spanish increasingly provides for our students a "passarelle" to the acquisition of both French and Italian since 2006, when the "French for Spanish Speakers" project was instituted by the French Cultural Services on our campus.[7] We have had the good fortune

---

[5] http://www.lasculturas.com/aa/aa070501a.htm
[6] See Randy Cordova, "Bellissima: Italian Singer a Favorite of Latinos," *The Arizona Republic*, July 16, 2006, http://www.azcentral.com/arizonarepublic/ae/articles/0716pausini0716.html, "Laura Pausini has become a major star in the Latin-music scene by sticking to her roots: She's an Italian-born singer whose music is overwhelmingly European-flavored pop. "I'm proud to be Italian," Pausini says, calling from her home in Milan. "But traveling around the world, Latin people give me the most passion and the most energy. They've treated me very respectfully and beautifully, and helped me to grow up."
[7] See Cécile Gregoriades, "Du Français pour les étudiants hispaniques de Long Beach," *Journal France-Amérique*, October 2010, p. 30; Clorinda Donato, Nicolas Bordage, and Philana Rustin, "French for

of collaborating with Professor Pierre Escudé, a linguist from the University of Toulouse, who is an expert in "Intercompréhension" or the intercomprehension of the Neolatin languages. Intercomprehension refers to "the spontaneous phenomenon of reciprocal understanding of related languages," as defined by Elisabetta Bonvino, Intercomprehension expert and co-author of *Eurom5. Leggere e capire 5 lingue romanze* (Hoepli 2011). Professor Escudé has spearheaded a number of projects funded by the European Union whose goals are to make Europe multilingual, especially when it comes to having speakers of one Neolatin language learn others.[8] He has helped us with course materials and the Intercomprehension thrust of our new "Italian for Spanish Speakers" course, taught for the first time during the Spring 2011 semester. My observation of this class offers insight into the depth and breadth of learning that can take place in the Intercomprehension classroom and the context for metalinguistic learning that it provides.

The instructor, Violetta Pasquarelli-Gascon, a Venezuelan teaching associate of Italian background, had thirty students following her every verbal and physical cue. They responded to her questions and asked questions themselves when they knew enough Italian to do so, but when they didn't, they asked, unabashedly in Spanish, or they translated with a word of English, and then went back to Spanish. Violetta began a new lesson with a beautiful PowerPoint on baroque architecture in Rome. "Ecco un magnifico esempio del barocco a Roma," Il barocco? Asked a student? " Cos'è il barocco?" "Es el barroco," replies her classmate, "Pero no comprendo barroco tampoco"... "The baroque" replied another student. "Che cos'è?" At this point, Violetta launched into a discussion of the characteristics of the baroque in Italian architecture. The students listened, nodded their heads and repeated its descriptors, "stravagante, bizzarro – il barocco, el barroco, the baroque." They nodded again with satisfaction. They had not only learned new vocabulary in Italian, but just as importantly, new content in not one, but three languages. The students were energized, validated and acutely aware that they were in a unique contact zone of multiple cultures and languages, one in which they

---

Spanish Speakers through Intercomprehension: A Method of Multiple-Language Acquisition for the Romance Languages with Implications for the Future," *ADFL Bulletin*, Vol. 42, No. 1 (2012), pp. 49-60.

[8] Pierre Escudé and Pierre Janin, *Le Point sur l'Intercompréhension, clé du plurilinguisme*, Cle Internationale, 2010.

were invited to use any of the "passarelles" available to them to move forward in their comprehension and acquisition.

In Fall, 2012 we added a second-year intensive hybrid course in Italian for Spanish speakers which filled beyond capacity (35 students). Our three-semester sequence of "Italian for Spanish Speakers" courses will be explored in greater depth in future publications.

Intercomprehension as concept and method opens doors for these students. Rather than wait for comprehensible input, they are empowered to use the input they already have to create and expand meaning. This is what it means to teach Italian to new audiences of language learners, students who come equipped with a rich foundation and heritage that allows them to move quickly into the "flow" of language and content acquisition that they are capable of reaching when the obstacles of other methods are removed.

From Pierre Escudé and the method of Intercomprehension, we have learned to be bolder in our expectations and to experiment with content and reading for accelerated acquisition and attainment of higher levels of competency in all four skills. Stories emerge in these classrooms, other immigrant stories. Italian migrations to Argentina, then to the United States—the trace of Italian sifted through multiple layers and languages, yet very much alive. Italian language, literature and culture become tools of recognition, renewal and innovation. I moved on with my observations in Spring 2011 to a second-semester class with ten students. Though it was not a course specifically organized for Spanish speakers, it turned out that all ten students were heritage speakers of Spanish. The instructor, Dr. Rossella Pescatori, noting their high level of comprehension, had prepared a lesson on the mind-body connection, using a provocative set of course materials. She moved from a discussion of how the mind and body are related, introducing vocabulary and concepts through popular songs, to a discussion of Italo Svevo's chapter from *The Conscience of Zeno,* "The Last Cigarette." She asked them what they thought of the reading. They lamented a bit over the level of difficulty encountered while reading the excerpt of Svevo's novel, but soon forgot about it, more interested in discussing Zeno and his psychological foibles, quirks they recognized immediately as being the plight of the overly aware modern individual who struggles with the fine line between pleasure and punishment. They recognized themselves in the character because the text was thoroughly "transparent" to them as speakers of Spanish reading Italian. These students "got it." They were also receptive to the follow-up lesson on who Svevo was and his place in Italian and world literature.

Why study Italian? These students will tell you why. Through Italian they find a validation of themselves, their language and culture, parallel values that work synergistically, leading to a better understanding of who they are and their place in the world. Their ability to relate to the cultural content of Italy and to find, through the study of Italian, a bridge both to Hispanic culture and the Spanish language, as well as to American culture and the English language, deserves special attention and reflection in a volume devoted to the importance of Italian language teaching in the United States today.

University administrators who work in the ever-growing numbers of Hispanic-Serving Institutions need to ask themselves what they are doing to fully harness the unique skill set of language and culture that Hispanic students bring to their classes. Sadly, this wealth of bicultural and bilingual knowledge often languishes, with no curricular outlet for its development and refinement. Around Italian, around Spanish, new identities, hybrid and, why not, Translatino, are being forged. These networks, new and evolving assemblages, to use Latour's terminology once again, establish pathways of flow to knowledge and translations of knowledge that are redefining the social and the individual in it.

STUDYING ITALIAN
A LINGUISTIC PERSPECTIVE

Professor Hermann W. Haller
Queens College and Graduate Center, CUNY

In most recent years the Italian language and culture have been enjoying a considerable popularity in the United States. Today, Italian is studied by some 81,000 students enrolled at colleges and universities across the U.S. (Fall 2009), from Alaska and Hawaii to New York and Massachusetts, with many more enrolled in High school or Middle and Elementary school courses, as well as in privately run programs. According to the most recent survey conducted by the Modern Language Association, Italian is the fourth foreign language studied at the college level, after Spanish, French, and German, with an increase of 3% since 2006.[1] At the global level, Italian appears to enjoy similarly a significant increase in popularity, as shown by the forthcoming survey *Italiano 2010* based on courses offered by 89 Italian Cultural Institutes. This survey claims a growth of 81% within ten years, from 3,548 to 6,429 courses.[2] The survey also lists as motivations for the study of Italian 1) Leisure and personal interest; 2) personal and family reasons; 3) work. Leisure and personal interest appeared as the dominant motivations given by North American respondents. In addition, the popularity of Italian is also seen in the increasing interest of travel to Italy, a country of numerous attractions, and in the large number of Study Abroad programs, especially in the cities like Florence and Rome.[3]

---

[1] For greater details see N. Furman, D. Goldberg, and N. Lusin, eds., *Enrollments in Languages Other Than English in United States Institutions of Higher Education, Fall 2009* (www.mla.org).
[2] For some pre-publication results see the article *L'inchiesta Italiano 2010. Anteprima di alcuni risultati* by its authors C. Giovanardi and P. Trifone, *Italiano LinguaDue* 2, 2010 (www.italianolinguadue.unimi.it). The survey aims at comparing data on courses offered at Italian Cultural Institutes with a similar survey conducted in the previous decade by T. De Mauro, M. Vedovelli, M. Barni and L. Miraglia, eds., *Italiano 2000. I pubblici e le motivazioni dell'italiano diffuse tra stranieri* (Rome: Bulzoni, 2002).
[3] Massimo Ciavolella refers to "la rinata moda del Grand tour," see Mario Calabresi's article in *La Repubblica*, 23 April 2007.

Naturally, proficiency in foreign languages and cultures broadens the mind of students, providing a window to alterity and allowing for greater interaction with an increasingly interconnected world.[4] The acquisition of a new language and culture furthers our appreciation of different social, anthropological, and historical fabrics. This is particularly true for Italy, with its enormous amount of artistic treasures and contributions to the world. Following are a few reasons in support of the sustained study and promotion of Italian in the U.S. from a linguistic perspective.

1. *Italian as a global language.* As the mother tongue of some 60 million speakers in Italy and Southern Switzerland, Italian is the language of one of the founding members of the European Union. As a Mediterranean language, Italian is also spoken as a second language in surrounding countries, from Albania and Croatia to Tunisia, due largely to past and present commercial interactions and to the media. It is also found throughout the world as a heritage language of people who emigrated from Italy, particularly in the late 19th and early 20th centuries and following World War II, but also throughout the most recent decades. The speakers of Italian abroad have been estimated to number 60 million, perhaps an inflated number, one that does not take into consideration different types and levels of proficiencies.

2. *Italian is the language of a great culture.* Throughout the world Italian and its dialects are appreciated as the languages of music with their suggestive vocalic resonance used in the opera, the canzone, and in the songs of contemporary musicians. It is also the language of Italy's arts, including painting, architecture, cinema, all with outstanding and often unparalleled traditions in European and global contexts. The numerous Italian loanwords in the English language alone – many imported during the Renaissance – reflect Italy's strong contributions to the arts. Italian is also the language of a great literature, of philosophical and scientific works. To mention just one example, Galileo wrote in Italian rather than in Latin to present his theories beyond the learned circles. Dante, Boccaccio, Petrarch, and Machiavelli are world literary figures whose works promoted a unitary language long before

---

[4] To cite but one telling case in point, in 2000 almost one of three New Yorkers spoke a LOTE (2,871,000 in a population of 8 million)(U.S. census).

the country's unification. Their masterpieces may be read by students with a good knowledge of modern Italian, as Tuscan lived for centuries mostly through the written tradition with relatively little change through time, if compared to languages such as French, English, or German.

Italian is a desirable language also beyond the realm of high culture, as it travels with the country's celebrated cuisine, fashion, and design, imitated and recreated throughout the world. Italian lives on the global palates with its *pizza, fettuccini, lasagna, prosciutto, espresso*, terms that for the most part have become Internationalisms. Not only are these Italian words commonly known by most Americans, Italian is also used to create gastronomic neologisms. In America's coffee culture we find creations such as *latte, venti macchiato, frappuccino,* and many others commonly used today.

Last but not least, Italy's great popularity and the history of cultural exchange with the Anglophone world is seen in the numerous Italian words used in the business world of urban areas, in the names of restaurants, as well as in a plethora of English loanwords that are ubiquitous in contemporary written and spoken Italian.

3. *Italian is a heritage language.* Today Italy has reached an unprecedented linguistic unity, with the Standard language spoken by the vast majority of its population at home and abroad, mostly in the form of regional varieties of Italian. One also finds a large number of dialects spoken both in Italy and abroad, from Sicilian and Neapolitan to Venetian and Sardinian. These varieties are gradually receding in the U.S. The recent American Community Survey (2008) suggests that there are now fewer than one million Americans above age 5 claiming to speak Italian at home.[5] Much of the Italian spoken in the community consists of forms of dialect speech that are gradually receding. However, as descendants from regional spoken Latin – not corruptions of Tuscan Standard –, Italy's dialects continue to be used by a majority of the country's population, mostly at home or among friends, in Italian-

---

[5] According to the American Community Survey of 2008 by the U.S. Census Bureau (Statistical Abstract of the United States, 2011, Tables 52 e 53) in a population of 17,749,000 persons of "Italian ancestry" 782,000 individuals above 5 years of age declared to speak Italian at home. See H. W. Haller, "Italoamericano" in *Enciclopedia dell'italiano*. Vol.1 (Rome, Istituto della Enciclopedia Italiana, 2010): 731-734.

ized forms, with code-switching with Italian, and with a distribution that differs across regions and social strata. The prevailing or exclusive use of dialects in Italy up to the second half of the last century was due in large part to the late political unification and numerous other factors, which restricted the use of the literary Tuscan based Standard to Tuscany and Rome, and to the educated classes. Unlike their frequently negative perceptions of the past, today the dialects are often celebrated as the languages of the family, the languages identifying individual roots. They are also widely studied by scholars. Perhaps not surprisingly, dialect words are a playful ingredient in texting and internet communication among the young whose dialect proficiency is passive or rudimentary at best, as well as in rap music and in advertising. In North America, especially in regions with large concentrations of heritage speakers (New York, New Jersey, Pennsylvania, and others) students of Italian are frequently confronted with dialects used by some of their peers, adding to the multilingual experience of contemporary classrooms. The study of Italian thus also provides a first-hand experience of the rich linguistic and cultural diversity of a country made up of regional cultures, all admired by a globalized citizenry. And because of the historically strong linguistic stratification and the presence of regional pronunciations of Italian, American students acquire the language in contexts that are relatively tolerant and free of purist constraints.

4. *Italian is a sister language of Spanish.* Spanish is the most frequently used non-English language in the U.S., attracting the largest number of students. Among the national languages that descend from Latin Spanish is most closely related to Italian in its linguistic structure. Spanish and Italian civilizations have interacted throughout history, with Spain's presence in Italy in past centuries, and with Italians migrating to Latin America, leaving their imprint especially in Argentina and Brazil. For mother tongue speakers of Spanish and heritage speakers of Spanish the study of Italian seems particularly attractive, as it leads to understanding two cultures spread respectively through colonization and peaceful labor migrations with their similarities and differences.

At a conference on the promotion of Italian held in Washington, D.C. more than a decade ago, Raffaele Simone proposed a number of reasons for sustaining Italian abroad through the creation of what he called a "virtual empire."[6] Among the forces contributing to a positive image (or mythology) of the Italian language he named immigration with an international vocation, investments in the European Union and the United Nations, the production of an international culture. Today this positive image has become a reality. For young people Italian is a desirable language, through travel, Study Abroad, cuisine, fashion, design, and the arts as powerful conduits.

In sum, Italian is the language of a seductive soft power, spread through a mostly invisible virtual empire. While not being the language of international communication or a dominant language in the Internet, it is the language of a culture that harbors enormous treasures, creative talent, and a great wealth of ideas. For American students it is a language of discovery of their identity, through the study of otherness, in a context in which ethnic diversity and stratification are increasingly common paradigms.

---

[6] Raffaele Simone, "Sette ragioni per sostenere l'italiano fuori d'Italia" in *Preserving and Promoting Italian Language and Culture in North America*, Gianclaudio Macchiarella, Hermann W. Haller, and Roberto Severino, eds. (Welland, Ont.-Lewiston, N.Y.: Soleil, 1997) 2-36.

Why I Studied Italian

Professor Fred Gardaphe
Distinguished Professor of English and Italian American Studies
Queens College & John D. Calandra Italian American Institute, CUNY

As a writer and professor of Italian American literature, I find knowledge of Italian essential not just for my work, but for my life. I, like many other grandchildren of immigrants, grew up listening to relatives, friends and neighbors speaking various dialects of Italian. I was pretty fluent in a language I thought was Italian. I studied Latin and Greek in high school, as Italian wasn't offered, but even had it been, I'm not sure I would have taken it as during that time I was trying to get as far away from being Italian as I could. It wasn't until I went to Italy for the first time, in 1979, that I realized if I were going to live my life to its fullest, I would have to know the language of my ancestors. That trip became a turning point in my life—the epiphany that made me realize I had to study Italian.

I arrived in Venice with what I thought was passable Italian. When the clerk at the hotel asked me if I preferred to speak English, I declined and was somewhat insulted. After all, wasn't I speaking Italian? His response was that whatever I was speaking, wasn't any Italian he had ever heard. Later, when I arrived in Castellana Grotte in Puglia, the home of my relatives, I was told I spoke like an old man and should go down to Piazza Garibaldi and speak to the pensioners that gathered there every day. I did and they all laughed at the young man who spoke the Castellanese of their youth. I returned home determined to learn Italian and in the process became a "born again" Italian.

That experience led me to focus my graduate school studies on Italian American literature and without fluency in Italian, I could never have accomplished all that I have in my career. In this brief essay I want to demonstrate the importance of knowing Italian. One of my key professional influences was Robert Viscusi, who in his essay, "De Vulgari Eloquentia: An Approach to the Language of Italian American Fiction," sets forth four categories of diction he found in Italian/American fiction. Viscusi's approach is modeled after Dante's *De Vulgari Eloquentia*, in which Dante calls for an

Italian that is "illustrious, cardinal, courtly and curial." In presenting the Italian/American counterpart to Dante's "eloquence," Viscusi calls for an eloquence that: "...must be able to change English in a way that will look Italian, that will in some way be Italian, no less indelibly than the writer's own name. It requires this property because of a purpose it shares with Dante's vernacular eloquence; it aims to suit the dignity of a nation that does not exist" (23).

Just as Dante had, "hoped to bring Italy into being by giving her a tongue fitted for the deliberations of her princes and judges," so do Italian/American writers hope to bring Italian America into being. But as Viscusi points out: "The American Italian's Italian American eloquence has aims that are slightly more diffuse. It does not wish to call a nation to sovereignty. Rather, it wishes to awaken Italian America to a sense of self, and then to console, to encourage, and to locate for this mythical nation a secure place that no one can confuse with is lost homeland or fabulous landfall" (23). And so, for fiction to be successfully Italian American, I realized that we must establish a critical basis for examining the language, and that work requires fluency in both languages.

There are many formal and contextual characteristics that make Italian/American literature different from the literature produced by other Americans. There are characters, themes, events, and rituals experienced by Italians that are recreated in the new country, and there are the concerns of language such as diction, dialect and word order that link the Italian American author to his or her ancestral culture. The first stage of my work examined the use of the Italian language in the fiction produced by Italian Americans. Later stages included examinations of the use of the Italian American dialect, themes and rituals. To establish a reference point for my discussion, I divided the body of Italian American literature I've examined into three chronological categories.

I started my observations by noting each and every time an Italian word, phrase and sentence was used. I came up with my numbers by counting each time an Italian word, phrase, or sentence appeared, even if it was repeated throughout the text. In fiction written by Italian Americans, the Italian language is most likely to appear in one or more of the following categories: Exclamations; Commands and direct address; *Parolacce* and *Bestemmie* (swear words); Proverbs; Foods and beverages or kitchen talk; Figurative language peculiar to Italians; Peculiar customs, dances, games, etc.; and Proper nouns: such as names and titles.

The initial observation I made, after charting the use of Italian in a sample of fifty Italian/American novels, was that the use of Italian has declined substantially over the years from 1924 to 1994. Since literature reflects the culture upon which it is based, this is not surprising. And since the use of the Italian language has declined over the past three generations, we should expect that its use by Italian/American writers would also decline. What is interesting is therefore not the quantity of the Italian words found in Italian/American novels, but the quality and the role or function that the Italian language plays as Italian American literature develops.

In the novels published between the years 1930 and 1955 the appearances of the Italian language are numerous. The amount of Italian found in these early novels suggests that these authors were very close to the Italian language.

During the Middle period, from 1955 to 1980 we begin to see a slight decrease in the number of appearances of Italian language in the fiction of Italian Americans. Helen Barolini's *Umbertina*, published in 1979, perhaps because of its length and epic quality contains the most Italian language of all. This novel provides a virtual first year grammar in the study of Italian. In *Umbertina* we find over 500 appearances almost equally distributed among all of the aforementioned categories. The Italian/American writing represented in this period reveals that the authors are still relatively close to the language.

It is during the period of 1980 to the present that we begin to witness a sharp decline in (in fact a near abandonment of) the use of Italian language by Italian/American authors. Most significant is the absence of complete sentences. A common characteristic of this group of writers is that the use of Italian is nearly restricted to fragments and single nouns. The use of Italian by younger writers has been reduced almost exclusively to the use of nouns which appear primarily in first generation character monologues and dialogues and rarely if ever in the narration. Thus, Italian for the younger writers clearly functions as a distance marker, demonstrating their greater distance from the language and its native speakers.

The words that most often appear with the greatest frequency in the writing of all three periods are the *bestemmie* and *parolacce*. Linguist Robert

DiPietro, in his essay, "Language as the Marker of Italian Ethnicity," provides some insight as to why this might happen.

> The Italian language, which was functional in every significant communicational network in the old country, can no longer be so here. For the Italian ethnic, it tends to become heavily invested with emotion. Strategic functions diminish and intimate social uses come to predominate. Jokes somehow become funnier when told in either Italian or with an Italian accent. Swearing seems more effective in Italian, even for some native-born American Italians. (205)

The tension in the search for identity of Italian Americans has always been a dominant theme in Italian/American fiction. Jerre Mangione has said that he wrote to create a third world, one in which he could feel he belonged. This cultural tension is reflected in the use of the Italian language by Italian/American writers – the tension between the independence of Italian words as they are presented individually by the more recent writers and the dependency of Italian words presented in sentences and phrases by their predecessors.

As Italian Americans lose the language of their ancestor, they lessen some of the tension this search for identity can create because there is a significant loss of one of the means of being identified with and connected to Italy. Think of the family as sentence and the individual as the word and you will have a clear picture of how Italian/American literature reflects its culture. To be American is to be dispersed, to move quickly and fragmented, to emphasize the individual in society, like the Italian used by younger Italian/American writers. To be Italian means to remain integral, to move slowly, to maintain the solidarity of the sentence, like the Italian used by the earlier Italian American writers. If Italian identity comes from name only, than individuals are nouns, disconnected from time and heritage.

My experience as a father has made me realize that nouns are the first parts of speech that a language learner masters and from my research it seems that nouns are last to disappear. Earlier generations of Italian/American writers used Italian in their lives and thus were more likely to use it in their writing. Later generations had heard the language and it became a part of their memory, but that memory is fragmented and shows us in pieces the

Italian part of the Italian American experience. The literature produced by a culture is also the preserved memory of that culture. Good literature helps the individual better understand him- or herself, because it connects them to the collective memory of humanity. Reading becomes a way of knowing the self. Fiction, by its very nature, creates myth, and the greater distance the author is from the Italian language, the more likely it is that the immigrant experience will be heroically or mythically presented.

What does this mean for writers of the next generation? Will their Italian/American characters become more mythic as the details fade? And what does this mean for the readers of the next generation? Will their search for an ethnic identity begin or end with the myth?

The Challenge

One way to maintain a heritage is to bind oneself to traditions by knowing literature. Italian/American literature can help Italian Americans find their culture and strengthen their identity. Not only does literature preserve what was lost through assimilation, it also preserves oral traditions as it creates a new context for the transmission of culture. If language transports culture, then loss of it could halt the progression of a culture. When language goes we must seek other means by which to identify with our ancestral heritage.

Richard Gambino, in an unpublished speech to Italian Americans on Columbus Day in Chicago many years ago, suggested that as we become more educated and as our family structure dissolves, we need to seek other means for learning about our culture. He suggests interaction with books, films and other indirect sources. I challenge our younger and future generations to not rely on those indirect sources, rather, to become direct sources themselves by learning the language, by studying history, and by connecting themselves to Italy through physical and mental travel to the land that for later generations has must become the "new" country. Italian/American writers and scholars have all dealt with the claim that Italian Americans do not read. Perhaps this idea comes from the fact that reading was given a low priority in the first generation's struggle for physical survival and in the second generation's struggle for adaptation to the American way of life. It is in our third generation, that we come across large numbers of Italian Americans who are looking to the past for a better understanding of their cultural roots.

Raised on the word, this group of third generation Italian Americans is the key to preserving, using, and creating written cultural documents. It seems that as the use of Italian disappears from our writers' vocabulary, their work becomes better accepted by American audiences, better than that of their predecessors. Though we have yet to replace our di Donato, Mangione, and Fante, we are witnessing today an increase in the number of Italian/American authors, whose books not only are published but also given attention in the review pages of local and national publications.

The Dream Book, edited by Helen Barolini was awarded a 1986 American Book Award. Tony Ardizzone's collection of short stories *The Evening News* was awarded a prestigious 1986 Flannery O'Connor award. Josephine Gattuso Hendin's *The Right Thing to Do* earned an *American Book Award*, as did Giose Rimanelli's *Benedetta in Guysterland*, 1993 American Book Award; both novels rejuvenate Italian/American literature through their use of Italian language. But Rimanelli, more than any other writer has turned his writing into a virtual primer of how to use Italian in American fiction. These are but a few of the writers who are more than ever before, being taken seriously by the dominant culture.

We have moved from being a primary oral culture, with little written literature, to being a literate culture with a diminishing oral context. It is time we too take our writers seriously by turning to our literature with a knowledge of Italian that will help us to know what it meant, means and will mean to be Italian American. And that means that we who care need to take back our past by studying and mastering the language not only of our ancestors, but those who live in the country our families left behind.

Italian as a Consumer Good

Cav. Silvana Mangione
Deputy Secretary General of CGIE
(General Council of Italians Abroad)

If it is true – and it is true indeed – that in the USA: "acquisition of knowledge is a consumer's good," how can we motivate an increasingly larger number of students to choose Italian as their second language, regardless of their ancestry and origin? Many people have given, described, and concocted a long list of reasons why everybody should study Italian. We will re-tell some of them and try to give additional suggestions.

The young Italian Delegates, who participated in the First Convention of Young Italians in the World, in 2008, wrote in their final document: "Identity is Language" and "Language is Culture." Both statements are fundamental and give us an insight into the way of thinking of our first emigration descendants. Italian is surely the language of those third, fourth and successive generations of Americans willing to reclaim an identity tie with the country of art and beauty par excellence. This is commendable and welcome, but it is not enough. Nostalgia or lack of knowledge of oneself, and heart-felt search for one's own "Ubi Consistam," do not constitute an inducement applicable to every American. We do not want to "ghettoize" the learning of Italian by limiting it to only one ethnic group within four hundred million citizens. Italian is the language of culture, music, art, history, and law; therefore, it should be studied by all those who aim at understanding in depth all fields of human endeavor.

This is unquestionable, but again it is not enough, because all areas of human genius can be learned from writings in other languages. Italian is the language of the country that – according to Americans – has the most refined sense of lifestyle, fashion, design, and food, and has made a business of them. Yes, but all of these aspects of living and trade can be enjoyed without speaking the language, just mastering the improbable pronunciation of "filosofia di vita, moda e cibo." The word "design" is normally used in Italy, and proves the unstoppable Anglicization of any idiom around the world, a phenomenon that should be contained, lest we lose forever the variety and richness of different forms of speech. Italian is the language of Opera. That cannot be denied, but it applies to opera buffs and career singers. It is not enough. Italian is the language of the most beautiful game in the world: soccer. Yes, but despite innumerable groups of soccer-moms, all subtleties of playing and collective insanity of aficionados can be expressed in English.

This too is not enough. None of these reasons can single-handedly convince all sorts of people to take Italian courses. Why, then, should Americans study Italian, starting from kindergarten and on, and on, and on? There is another reason, which is not often considered, even if it is or should be decisive. From a linguistic point of view, Italian is a "synthetic" language, while English is an "analytic" one. With the conjugation of verbs and the endings and gender of nouns, singular and plural, feminine and masculine, in Italian there is no need to use personal pronouns and possessive adjectives to make the listener understand what is being said. Therefore, by studying, speaking, reading and writing Italian, we give our brain a new and different way of organizing our thoughts, a distinct approach to problem solving, and a separate tool of deliberation. If our brain were a Ferrari, we would say that by learning Italian we give it one additional, winning gear. It could be argued that Spanish and French also have a similar linguistic structure. Certainly, but they do not carry the harmony and musicality of the most beautiful language in the world. Spanish offers the harsh and inhaled sounds of castanets and hidalgos. The French tongue explodes its grandeur through the nose and throat. That does not apply to the Italian language, which sings of the beauty surrounding it, the beauty that Italy created without interruption from prehistoric times to today. Italy is the only country on earth that has never stopped producing masterpieces, which amount to over 65% of the world's total, according to UN statistics. Perhaps Italy would have not succeeded in offering this feast to mankind, if the progression from Latin to the language of Dante Alighieri and Umberto Eco had not been accompanied by a gradual, continued choice of sweeter, more lyric or more onomatopoeic sounds for its vocabulary. Italian has even absorbed words imposed by centuries of invasions, adapted them to our melodious speech, and returned them to the herds of foreigners, who conquered us, subduing them with our elegant way of signifying diverse concepts and objects.

These motivating suggestions are rarely, if at all, mentioned, but are probably the most relevant in a system intent on building culture not as dry information, but as profound enlightenment and awareness of oneself and of one's future becoming: an Italianization process that is a must in the times we live in, increasingly less conscious of individual values and evermore enslaved by second-rate practices of loud individualism.

CONSUMING IN ITALIAN
NOURISHMENT OF THE MIND

Lidia Bastianich
Lidia's of Italy

It is not unusual for me to walk down the street and be approached by my fans telling me: "Lidia we love your cooking show" or "Lidia, I love it when you say at the end of the show "Tutti a Tavola a Mangiare." Often when I am at book signings I am asked to write an Italian message in the book: *buon appetito, mangia e cucina italiana, buon compleanno*. I am amazed by all the emails of appreciation I receive when I use Italian words on the show, and translate them into English. I am truly honored by the attention and the following of my viewers, customer and fan base and am grateful for how much the American people love Italian food, Italian food products and the Italian family lifestyle. Lidia's Italy, my Public Television cooking show is one of the most popular cooking shows in the U.S., available in 96% of American households and receives incredibly high ratings. Public Television represents what America is watching, and America is watching Italian cultural programming.

My Italian restaurants have a great following as well, and my Italian cookbooks are best sellers. All indications in my professional and personal experience are that the American people love Italian food and all things Italian and are eager to learn and assimilate as much as possible what is Italian and what will enrich their family, their table, and beautify their home and lives.

Mangia! Ciao, bella! Gelato! Arrivederci! are Italian phrases commonly used in the American culture today, and most likely picked up during a visit to the splendid peninsula, frequenting Italian restaurants, viewing Italian movies, meeting Italian friends, shopping in Italian stores, and listening to Italian music. The language of music is also very Italian: *allegro, andante, poco a poco, vivace, moderato, staccato*, words from any other language would just not fit it the word of music so beautifully. There are Italian food words that have become part of the American vernacular. What other name would you call spaghetti by, but spaghetti? And, is it not important to know that the word for string is *spago* in Italian and hence spaghetti, or little strings. Most American people feel very comfortable in ordering ossobuco in a restaurant, and know exactly what they are ordering; the word has become part of the American culture. The actual veal cut is the shank bone or *osso*, which when cut ends up with a hole or *buco* in the center, which is what ossobuco means in Italian. Is it truly enough to know *al dente* and *alla parmigiana*? When a culture is loved as much by the American people as the Italian culture, should there not be proper opportunities in learning institutions and make it accessible for children and adults alike to be able to learn Italian?

When I arrived in America in 1958 with my family, as a young girl of twelve, I did not speak English, but I knew that I wanted to be part of the American culture as soon as I could. The first thing was to learn the language and that I did in six months. A language is not just a means of communication; it is the colors, sounds, and tastes of a culture and its people. The studying of any language opens a window onto that culture.

Italian is the language of some of the world's finest literature, extraordinary musical pieces and operas. It is the menu for a favored ethnic cuisine and the language for some of arts greatest movements. It is the language that belongs to the country that has the largest number of UNESCO World Heritage sites and is the 5th most visited country in the world. The study of Italian, a Latin root language, provides the young with a rich vocabulary skill set and a musical language with high pitched i's and rolling r's. IT IS Indeed, a language and culture that has much to add to young developing minds and enrichment to anyone's life.

Why Study Italian?

Cav. Vincenzo Marra
ILICA

Because it is the language of harmony and it sounds like a melody when well spoken.

However, in a world of pragmatism and efficiency framed by high technology, who needs the sound of music? – The human race needs it! Italian is the language of humanistic culture inspired by the beauty of art, by the harmony of creation…. Stop right here: "Does it produce profit intended as money?" – Of course and it also enriches who choose to learn Italian by amplifying their knowledge of history way back to the birth of western civilization.

Far from the usual rhetoric, the Italian language is an essential tool to a better understanding of the identity of the western world. From the banking system to the study of space, from the discovery of America to the modern constitution, the Italian language represents the best tool to read music, medicine and art.

In the 1700 the Italian language was more popular than the English language today. Matteo Ricci was the first to translate Chinese ideograms into Latin language then Italian. Suddenly Italy appears to be out of fashion as new products and new languages become more attractive for life and business, thus tools for profit. From window shopping to restaurants, the world continues to speak Italian.

We believe, however, that the Italian language is valued as a precious asset by those who understand all the above concepts: the "Italophiles" or those who love Italy, its history and its culture. The traditional American of Italian origin insists to be named to promote the Italian language and culture with a superficial knowledge of either one of them. And it is a known fact that a good salesman must know first the product he sells to be credible. I.L.I.C.A. Italian Language Inter-Cultural Alliance has introduced the Intercultural Italian language promotional concept. Chinese, Middle Easterners, Koreans,

Americans and all the emergent cultures of the XXI century must study Italian to better understand the history of our planet. The White House has recommended for every American to learn a second language in order to better understand the New World Order. We wish that all Americans will learn Italian as a second language. Americans of Italian origin are welcome!

Perché è la lingua dell'armonia e sembra di ascoltare una melodia quando è ben parlata.

Comunque nel mondo del pragmatismo e dell'efficienza condizionati dall'alta tecnologia, chi ha bisogno della musica? – Il genere umano! L'Italiano è la lingua della cultura umanistica ispirata dalla bellezza dell'arte e dall'armonia della creazione… Un momento, ma la lingua Italiana produce profitto inteso come denaro?" – Certamente, e arricchisce coloro che scelgono di studiarla amplificando la conoscenza della storia fin dalla nascita della cultura occidentale. Lungi dal cadere nella trappola della retorica, sottolineamo l'importanza della lingua Italiana come strumento essenziale per comprendere l'identità della cultura occidentale. Dal sistema bancario allo studio dello spazio, dalla scoperta dell'America alla moderna costituzione, la lingua Italiana rappresenta il migliore strumento per leggere la musica, la medicina e l'arte. Forse pochi sanno che la lingua Italiana era nel 1700 più popolare di quanto non lo sia oggi la lingua Inglese. Matteo Ricci fu il primo a tradurre in Latino gli ideogrammi Cinesi che furono poi trasferiti in Italiano.

Oggi viviamo in un periodo dove l'Italia sembra aver perso la priorità, nelle scelte del mondo, di cui godeva fino al secolo scorso. Nuovi prodotti e nuove lingue vengono preferite all'Italiano come strumenti per scambi commerciali e profitti economici.

Eppure noi continuiamo a credere che la lingua Italiana, dopo l'Inglese, mantenga obiettivamente il proprio valore di patrimonio internazionale: dalle vetrine alla ristorazione, il mondo continua a parlare anche Italiano. E la lingua Italiana resta comunque un vantaggio prezioso per coloro che comprendono i concetti fin qui espressi: gli Italofili e tutti coloro che amano l'Italia, la sua storia e la sua cultura. L'Americano medio di origine Italiana insiste a voler essere il promotore della lingua Italiana dimostrando scarsa conoscenza della stessa lingua e della cultura. Un buon venditore deve conoscere il prodotto che vende per essere credibile.

I.L.I.C.A., Italian Language Inter-Cultural Alliance, ha introdotto il concetto della promozione interculturale della lingua. Cinesi, Arabi, Coreani, Americani e tutte le culture emergenti del XXI secolo devono studiare l'Italiano per meglio comprendere la storia del nostro pianeta. La Casa Bianca ha raccomandato che gli Americani imparino tutti una seconda lingua per meglio comprendere il nuovo ordine mondiale. Noi vogliamo che ogni Americano parli Italiano come seconda lingua. Gli Americani di origine Italiana sono benvenuti!

"Prima Cominci, Meglio è"
The Sooner You Start, The Better.

Cav. Berardo Paradiso
Italian American Committee on Education, President

In any country, like the United States, where global communication and a global economy are now prevalent, studying a foreign language should be mandatory in every elementary school.

IACE, the Italian American Committee on Education, is there to promote the teaching of Italian in the K-8th grade levels of the public and catholic schools in the Tri-State area of New York, New Jersey, and Connecticut.

With my profession in international business, and as President of IACE, I strongly believe that any citizen who wants to be part of this competitive global world has to be articulate in at least one other language. In order to acquire fluency, years of study are necessary, which is why a child should be exposed to a foreign language at an early age.

Many studies, one of which was performed by the College Board, have examined the benefits of studying another language: foreign language students, after at least four years, scored higher in their SAT's (Scholastic Aptitude Test) than those who had studied four years or more in any other subject. Based on this study, the Superintendent of the New Rochelle Schools (NY) started a pilot bilingual Spanish-English teaching program in one of the elementary schools. The students enrolled in this program would later score the highest grades in any other subject area.

Encouraged by these results, we, at IACE, invested in collaboration with the New Rochelle school district to start a similar dual program with Italian at the pre-K level. It has been only three years since we implemented this program, and we are discovering amazing results: every child enrolled is already fluent in both Italian and English, and shows increased interest in other subjects.

There is a scientific explanation for this: Dr. Andrea Michelli, a well-known, respected scientist at the Institute for Cognitive Neuroscience at the University College in London, completed a research project showing that one's brain gains density and elasticity, as well as gray matter, by being bi- or multilingual. Brain research in Canada has confirmed Dr. Michelli's study, adding that individuals highly proficient in a second language show a slower decline in mental power with age.

The Advanced Placement Italian program has been re-introduced in the USA schools thanks to all of the Italian associations, authorities, and the concerned Italian community, who have courageously fought for it and its financing. The AP level in any subject matter is very high and rigorous, but also an asset for students and parents in order to save time and money, since a high score on the AP earns a student college credits.

One condition for enrollment and success in a language AP course mostly relies on the length and adequacy of the preparation beforehand: language students should arrive at the AP level fluent in their speaking, listening, and writing skills. This is one more reason, and actually an essential one, for starting children early on a language; it is the most natural way, the same way we all learn how to speak our mother tongue.

But why Italian as a second language?

The 2000 Census registered 17,749 million Americans of Italian ancestry. The Tri-State area – New York, New Jersey and Connecticut – in which IACE has been active, is the most heavily Italian-American area: 14,8% in New York, 18,5% in New Jersey, and 19,8% in Connecticut.

Many Italian-Americans of the third, fourth or fifth generation want to go back to their roots through learning the language of their background. Speaking Italian will help them get back in touch with even remote relatives, visit their places of origin, and be more warmly welcomed and understood by them. Speaking the language of one's ancestors and transmitting it to one's children will preserve and maintain one's background culture, values, and traditions.

Italy is today's most visited country in the world, for its natural beauty, welcoming people, art (More than 60% of the world art!), fashion, and cuisine. Being able to speak its language makes the whole traveling experience even more rewarding and enriching.

Knowing Italian automatically leads to understanding the Italian culture and appreciating it here at home: just think of how one can appreciate the lyrics of Puccini's *Madama Butterfly* or any other Italian Opera if one speaks and understand Italian! Likewise, one can better savor the images and the story in *Cinema Paradiso* if one doesn't have to read the (often approximate) subtitles to grasp the meaning!

More than 50% of English word roots come from Latin. Learning Italian helps understand and master one's own language, as well as scientific or legal names or nouns. It becomes a real advantage for word power in the SAT!

There are many possibilities for students of Italian to further their studies in Italy and get degrees at Italian universities. A deeper, first-hand education about the country and its culture, and acquired expertise at the language will be assets instrumental to one's career back home, whether in teaching or in any other field relating to Italy.

With the expansion of the industrialization of Italy within the last thirty years, there are numerous business opportunities for trade between the U.S. and Italy. Within this global economy, being able to speak Italian will be an asset to creating better communication and to acquiring speedier results. It is a tool for establishing continuity in relations and a guarantee for success.

We live in a fast, technologically borderless culture, where the Internet, Facebook, Twitter, and other social arenas have given us the platforms through which to share ideas with the world instantaneously and to bring about immediate results: the best examples in this regard are the recent Tunisian and Egyptian revolutions. If their youth had not been able to communicate their anger to the world in English – to them a foreign language – their ideas and actions might not have had the same impact.

Today's parents have a duty, which they cannot ignore: our society will be increasingly more globalized and competitive. Its future depends on how well our children will be prepared to be open to other cultures. One of the best ways to know, accept, and relate to another culture is to know its language.

Fashion and Translation
The Global Language of Italian Style

Professor Eugenia Paulicelli
Queens College and the Graduate Center, CUNY

During the 2012 Super Bowl, the biggest national television event in the US, which draws millions of Americans to watch the game with family and friends accompanied by Super Bowl food – nachos, beer, potato chips and the like – something new and Italian happened that captivated the multi-million strong audience. The unexpected television event was the sexy ad for the new FIAT 500 Abarth, recently launched on the American market. In Italy, of course, the icon of Italy's reconstruction during the so-called economic boom was the Cinquecento. Now it makes its reappearance, not as a family car, but as a vehicle that appeals to consumers of sophisticated taste. In the video, which became a big hit on YouTube, we see a nerdy type who obviously pays little attention to his appearance walking in the street drinking a cappuccino, a young man on a little break from his desk. He is immediately struck (like a *colpo di fulmine* we say in Italian) by the vision of a gorgeous woman wearing a sleeveless silk black and red dress and high heels. These are the same colors as the car we see later. The model who played the woman is Catrinel Menghia, born in Romania, but presently living in Milan where she is married to former soccer player Massimo Brambati. In the ad she speaks Italian with a very slight accent, almost unnoticeable. The woman epitomizes Mediterranean, but yet modern and offbeat beauty. Thinking the man is ogling her, she goes up to him and says: "Che cosa guardi? Mi stai spogliando con gli occhi…" Looking at her now from behind, we see she has a small and cute tattoo on the back in the shape of a scorpion. The last thing she says to him is "Ti senti perso pensando che potrei essere tua per sempre?" The man, who is a good bit shorter than the model, and is completely overwhelmed by her beauty, now wakes up from this beautiful dream. We see him now kissing the new FIAT 500 instead of the young woman. Next, the ad shows us the

500 on the road and we hear in English: "Fiat 500 Abarth. You will never forget the first time you see one."

There are a few things that are interesting in this ad and that connect some threads that I would like to comment on. One is the language. During prime time, in the middle of the television event of the year, when a 30 second ad costs a fortune, we hear only Italian, maybe a first in the history of Super Bowl advertising. Secondly, this ad epitomizes some of the most enduring auras that are associated with Italian identity: beauty, style, and design. Not to mention a strong hint of sexiness and warmth. Thirdly, the connection, typical of advertising and the imaginary in general, of putting together fashion and cars, fashion and design, fashion and status. It is with these three points in mind that I would like to talk about Italian fashion.

Fashion as a manufacturing industry and a symbolic force is and has always been a meeting place of cultures, aesthetics, habits that interact with each other (either in conflict or cooperation). This relationship is inevitable and it is what defines fashion via trade, commerce, migration, travel, whether virtual or real. In fact the Fiat ad could be considered just such an example of the cross-cultural translation of Italian fashion and style. Objects and garments continue their life and journey when they are lived and worn. The result is a global vernacular sprinkled with local flavor and a personal touch. The making of this process of assemblage is also a process of translation. Think, for instance, that sometimes what we have selected to wear before a journey and for a certain occasion becomes obsolete when we reach the destination (not only for climatic reasons). We inhabit place and space differently each time we change landscape, color, flavor, habits, taste, and the way we perceive that particular space and place. Clothing is one of the vectors of the way we negotiate and translate our being in and between worlds and cultures that speak to each other.

Clothing, accessories and ornaments that adorn the body are made to be transferred and to migrate from one body to another, one locale to another, one country and one continent to another. Difference, repetition and change define the rhythms of fashion and desire. The Fiat ad, while embodying the exchange of languages, also aims at creating a global vernacular with which everyone can identify. What is of interest to us is that here the Italian language is used as if it were English, today's lingua franca.

Fashion is a language whose meanings are transmitted through visual language. The appeal of a wearable object, dress or accessory has the power to project identity. Very often in the US, wearing Italian clothing means that one wants to wear and embody the architecture, the beauty and art of Italy or speak the language. Indeed, choosing the right clothes can transform one's appearance. In fact, the literature from the Italian Renaissance that codified good "taste" gave precise instructions to its readers about how to look good. Here resides fashion's power and seductiveness. Moving on a century or so from the Renaissance, it is worth recalling that fashion magazines of the 1950s and 1960s often featured advertisements for cars accompanied by the perfect dress to match the color, style, and level of income of the presumed buyer. A car was paired with the right dress. The 50s and 60s were a time of a profound urban economic and cultural transformation both in the US and Italy.[1] It was also the time in which more and more Americans visited Italy and fell in love with it. The American magazine *Harper's Bazaar* in 1960 published a photo story promoting Ford, the American car company. The photo shoot was called "Rome loves Ford, Ford loves Rome." The text features the creations of two Rome-based fashion houses, Fontana and Gattinoni, along with two red suits where the color red is associated with Rome (an early edition of the "Valentino Red" of more recent years). The models are two Roman aristocrats described in the captions. Later, the Fontana Sisters' "easy suit decision" and Gattinoni's buttonless jacket over a pink satin blouse matching the jacket's lining were copied by David Crystal for Saks and sold for $110. In the growing Fordist economy, cars became the foremost symbol of progress and, of course, served the new need for social mobility that informed the urban revolution. It is precisely at this time that suburbs and shopping malls began to appear in the US, reconfiguring space.[2]

In the *Harper's Bazaar* case above, it was Ford that was marketing its campaign in Italy, one of the many signs of the "Americanization" of Western European countries. In a similar vein, the Fordist economy in Italy correctly perceived the central role of vehicles. What is interesting to note, however, is that the codes governing objects and society are subject to change. The return

---

[1] Antonio Maraldi and Eugenia Paulicelli eds., *1960. Un anno in Italia. Costume. Cinema, Moda e Cultura* (Cesena: Società Editrice Il Ponte Vecchio, 2010).
[2] David Harvey, *The Condition of Postmodernity* (London: Blackwell, 1990), and his subsequent study, *Spaces of Capitals. Towards a Critical Geography* (New York: Routledge, 2001).

of the Fiat 500 in our postmodern globalized and wired world assumes a completely different meaning from that of the 1950s and 1960s. But this also tells us that the complex process of translation and the reuse of the past in new forms are at the core of fashion as a manufacturing industry and as a powerful symbolic force. The process of transformation inherent in fashion is also triggered by migration. In the 1950s and 1960s, Italian migration to Anglo-American countries brought with it new culinary and sartorial flavors. In fact, In January 2006 the British paper *The Guardian* published a special feature that mapped the many ethnic groups who have settled in the different neighborhoods of London, named as one of the most ethnically diverse and multicultural cities of the world. In one of these accounts I found a fascinating detail: the role Italian immigration to the UK and especially to London in the early sixties had in the creation of the Swinging Sixties. As the *Guardian* article says:

> Many of the thousands of southern Italians who arrived in London in the 1950s and 1960s settled in Soho – then a cheap part of town – and found work running cafes and restaurants. The impact on the locals was tremendous: spaghetti and espresso – and Ferrari and Fellini – had a deep effect on a generation of Londoners looking for something more sophisticated than brown Windsor and bowler hats. It was from this Italian-driven scene that the idea of London as a stylish, cosmopolitan and, eventually, swinging city was formed. (01-21-05)

A similar impact on male suits was made on the youth tribe known as the "mods," who sported an Italian style of dress and rode their Vespas in the streets of London. What is interesting in this article is that it highlights how an immigrant group contributed to modernizing and transforming the flavor of a city. Similar phenomena, I am sure, can be found in many other cities in the world. Everyone, I am sure, has seen how Starbucks has coined a myriad of variations on coffee and cappuccino, the two classical Italian beverages. In the language of Starbucks, "wet cappuccino" means a cappuccino with a "little foam"; "Grande" defines the size of the coffee without any need of the English translation; the people making the copy are called *baristi*; and a cookie is a *biscotti* (this is plural in Italian, but singular in Starbucksspeak)

So it is important to study the history of Italian fashion and the language of Italian fashion in an interdisciplinary setting and in a global perspective, and with any eye to its links to cinema, literature, art and digital technology. This study could be both an appealing and rich opportunity to understand the economic, cultural and social transformations of the Italian nation. But it would also serve to train students to become cognizant of the contemporary world and equip them with the necessary critical and historical skills to understand the world they live in and its history. This could also be a pedagogical tool for teaching Italian language and culture in the US and give an opportunity to explore the history of Italy in a global context.

How would it be possible to understand the industrial revolution in 19th-century England without connecting it to textile manufacturing? In the Renaissance, for instance, Italian cities such as Venice, Lucca, Naples, and others were important centers for the production of textiles and luxury goods that were demanded by an ever-growing consumer society. But it is also true that textiles and fabrics bear the signs of a continuous flow and exchange process that is today accelerated because of the pace of digital technology. Public spaces, such as shops and shopping malls, museums, window displays, soap operas, film, blogs and websites create the conditions for longing and create new forms of performativity. Think, for instance, of the close link between film and fashion and how these two industries and art forms have been feeding off each other since the beginning of the medium and continue to do so. In the US, for instance, some of the most popular fiction serials, which are also broadcast in Italy, such as *Glee* and *Gossip Girl* corroborate the power of celebrities to influence consumption choices and taste. Teen-age girls and young women can purchase on line the brands of clothing and accessories worn by the characters of these (and many other) shows. Internet users can easily access each and every one of the characters and undress him or her to have a peek at the labels of the clothes they wear and browse the internet, window shopping – screen-shopping might be better – and with just a click order the desired garment and look. Fashion and dress are pervasive because they affect us in the way we are perceived in public space or in the way we feel about ourselves. Digital technology has contributed to bring to the fore these issues of identity related to public appearance and has redefined the private spaces by connecting individuals and communities that would otherwise remain disconnected. It brings the far away closer. It is more necessary than ever to navigate real and virtual spaces with the appropriate attire and equipped with the appropriate critical tools. The world has become smaller and infinitely bigger at the same time. And yet Italian fashion has maintained a cultural cachet. Aesthetics and creativity have been integral components of the image of Italian sensibility. In the 1980s, the aesthetic dimension went hand in hand with the glamorized image of Italy that was projected through fashion and style and which has since become one of the strongest, if not the strongest, image foreigners have of things Italian. It is not by chance that this phenomenon coincided with the emergence of the "Made in Italy" label, the national trade brand that incarnated all the allure and elegant design characteristic of Italian products. Commenting on fashion's national role, Peppino Ortoleva has pointed out how fashion has the power to orient potential customers "towards one country or another and (even more frequently) toward one aspect or another of a national image, inasmuch as it makes the public feel intimately contemporary."[3] As a consequence of this complex process, Ortoleva adds, fashion has a great impact over time on the construction of both a stable and flexible repertory of images and mythologies with which one wishes to identify, belong and buy into. This kind of perspective is confirmed by John Agnew when he notes that fashion takes an active role in "Spatializing the world – dividing, labeling and sorting it into a hierarchy of places of greater or 'lesser' importance."[4] This mechanism has grown especially visible in the last two decades, as fashion has become an ever more powerful and desirable element of cultural capital for the cities of the world. Fashion becomes and is one of the most powerful motors driving the big tourist industry machine. In this Italy can play one of its strongest cards, especially if it is accompanied by the right promotional campaign geared towards support for the rich artisanal tradition without which Italian style would not be possible, combined with advanced technology and creative/innovative design. This is a project that cannot limit itself to solely propagandistic aims, but needs to draw on the interconnectedness and

---

[3] Peppino Ortoleva, "Buying Italian: Fashions, Identities, Stereotypes," in Giannino Malossi, ed., *Volare. The Icon of Italy in Global Pop Culture* (New York: Monacelli, 1999) 46-54.

[4] John Agnew, *Geopolitics. Re-visioning World Politics.* (London: Routledge, 1998); David Gilbert, "From Paris to Shanghai. The Changing Geographies of Fashion's World Cities," in Christopher Breward and David Gilbert eds., *Fashion's World Cities.* (Oxford: Berg, 2006).

support of the institutions (schools, university, industry etc.) both in Italy and abroad that understands fashion in its global significance and context.

The FIAT Super Bowl spot confirms that although Italy has gone through a complex phase of transformation in the age of globalization, and migrations, there is still a strong message that fashion, Italian style is able to convey and that it still has a hold on the imagination for foreigners, especially for Americans.

The ad also tells us that things Italian are still sexy; that Italian taste and style have visually and verbally colonized foreign territories, even the territories of the great colonizers. What it is important to bear in mind is that identity and style are not entities that are fixed once and for all, they do not mean the same thing all over the world. It is our task to make sure that beauty, the high skilled of artisanal work (the Italian hand) are preserved and that new research and creativity in the field of fashion and design is encouraged, fostered and supported. Many Italian brands have been able to marry tradition with innovation, as in the case of Cucinelli in Umbria or the Neapolitan tailors represented in the recent documentary *O'Mast* (2011) by Gianluca Migliarotti. There is a lot of work, but exciting work, ahead of us.

Study Abroad in Italy

Professor Roberto Dolci
Università per Stranieri di Perugia

The Advantages of Studying Abroad

Is there a difference between studying the History of the Roman Empire in Rome, Italy or in Rome, Georgia?[1] What do Americans like Theodore Roosevelt, Bill Clinton and Condoleezza Rice have in common; Nobel Prize winners such as James Watson and Milton Friedman; writers and poets like Rita Dove, Sylvia Plath and John Irving; U.S. representatives and senators like Rosa Di Lauro, Carl Albert and Max Burns and many others who assumed leadership roles in the arts and letters, science, medicine, education, business, communications, and government? At least one thing: they all studied abroad.

Even though less than 1% of U.S. students study abroad for credits, they are nonetheless good travelers overall. About half of them traveled outside the U.S. at least once. The vast majority went on holidays, for a period of less than two weeks. They are more and more interested in what is happening in the world and they consider going abroad an important experience. These are the conclusions of a study published in 2001 by the American Council of Education (Hayward & Siaya 2001).

Sometimes parents are reluctant to send their children abroad to study, not only because of the cost, but also because they think it is a waste of time.

The students themselves underscore the costs, the concern for an academic career, the lack of knowledge of the language, various family and personal obstacles, and the lack of interest among the reasons for not studying abroad (Hayward & Siaya 2003).

Those who went abroad declare that such an experience was useful and important for their education. Among the benefits, students identify the expansion of knowledge, that the experience made them become more mature, that it is the best way to learn a foreign language and that they are more

---

[1] Adapted from Bolen 2006.

competitive in the labor market (Hayward & Siaya 2001).

Many scholars who have studied the impact of study abroad on employers and employees confirm these results. A period abroad and the use of foreign languages had a major impact on their future careers as employees (Norris and Gillespie 2009).

Studies (Trooboff Van De Berg, Ryman 2008) (Tilman et al. 2005) show that among the factors that employers consider most important when hiring a person are social skills, the ability to communicate successfully in intercultural contexts, the ability to work effectively even in uncomfortable situations, and the aptitude to evaluate and interpret situations.

For employers, a person who has spent a period of study abroad has developed leadership skills, autonomy, flexibility and maturity (Orahood, Kruze, Easley Pearson 2004). Understandably, the more is an international company the more a learning experience abroad is considered important (Trooboff, Van De Berg, Ryman 2008).

Similarly, students say that spending time abroad gives them more job opportunities. "Interestingly, alumni also believe that a degree with an international component or a full degree from an overseas university would be just as attractive as, if not more attractive than, a degree from a U.S. university, to employers" (Thompson 2003).

Studying abroad also improves academic achievement without slowing down progress to degree, as many parents and students believe. In 2010 the results of a ten-year longitudinal study assessing study abroad program outcomes in the 35 institutions comprising the University of Georgia system were made public. The results speak clearly:

> [S]tudents who study abroad have improved academic performance upon returning to their home campus, higher graduation rates, and improved knowledge of cultural practices and context compared to students in control groups. [S]tudying abroad helps, rather than hinders, academic performance of at-risk students (Sutton, Rubin 2010).

Thus studying abroad offers personal and professional advantages. It is a moment of personal growth: the opportunity to be in contact with people from other cultures and speak other languages develops a cultural awareness that allows everyone to better understand his/her own culture. This occurs through an internal and external dialogue that allows people to see things from different perspectives. Understanding others helps us to better understand ourselves.

Why Study in Italy

The number of American students who studied abroad has grown tremendously in recent years. The number of students has more than tripled, from about 80,000 in 1990 to about 270,604 in 2010. However, this number represents less than 1% of students enrolled in college (IIE 2011).

The study areas mostly covered are the Social Sciences (20.7%), Business and Management (19.5%), Humanities (12.3%), Fine or Applied Arts and Physical/Life Sciences (7.3%) and Foreign Language (6.1%) (IIE 2011).

Among the geographical regions students select, Europe is chosen by half of American students, Latin America by 15% and Asia by 12% (IIE 2011).

The most popular countries are The United Kingdom with 32,683 students, accounting for 12.1%, Italy with 27,940 students representing 10.3% of the total, followed by Spain, France, China, Australia and Germany (IIE 2011).

As already mentioned, statistics show that in 2010 Italy is second only to Britain among the destinations chosen by American students. It is the first non-English speaking country preferred. The trend has grown over the last twenty years: since 1985, Italy has climbed the rankings from fourth to second place, with an increase of 2.1% over the previous year, (IIE 2011). Why this success?

Economically, in 2011 imports from Italy recorded an increase of 19.17% compared to 2010. The total value was 33,968 billion dollars. In the first half of 2012 there was a further increase of 9.55%. All economic sectors are involved: the first three are mechanics, fashion, and food. Italian companies in the USA number 1206,[2] while American companies in Italy include some 560.[3]

---

[2] Ambasciata d'Italia a Washington, "Cooperazione Economica," http://www.ambwashingtondc.esteri.it/Ambasciata_Washington/Menu/I_rapporti_bilaterali/Cooperazione_economica/, accessed July 2012.
[3] American Chamber of Commerce in Italy, http://www.amcham.it/, accessed July 2012.

From the cultural and artistic point of view, Italy currently has the largest number of sites included in the list of UNESCO World Heritage Sites: 44 artistic and 3 environmental.[4]

From the social point of view, in 2010 more than 17 million Americans claimed to have Italian ancestors.[5]

These economic, cultural, and social data might already be adequate to explain why Italy is the second most preferred destination for study abroad. Italy has a long tradition as a destination for U.S. students. In 1956 *Italica*, the AATI journal published a paper designed to provide useful information to American students who wanted to study in Italy. The reason was thoroughly well explained at the beginning of the article:

> Each year more American students travel to Italy to take advantage of the heritage of fine educational and cultural benefits which have drawn foreigners to its schools for centuries. It is no wonder that there has been an increase in the educational exchange programs between the two countries. Annually about $600,000 is spent for this purpose." (Pastenok 1956, 286)

At the end, the author clearly states that it is necessary for students to take a course in Italian language. "Only then can they be adequately equipped to enjoy and appreciate the beauty and endless opportunity which Italy offers" (Pasternok 1956, 290).

We have previously described the benefits in terms of personal and professional growth afforded by spending some time abroad. We should also consider how developing knowledge of the language and culture being studied is also a plus. In 1956 it was difficult to receive authentic and up-to-date materials to study the Italian language, to have opportunities for contacts, and to dialogue with native speakers, not to mention organizing a trip to Italy. Nowadays, thanks to the development of digital technology, it is possible to be in constant contact with Italy and to receive daily information about what is happening. However, immersing oneself in everyday life where the language is spoken and the culture lived provides a considerable impetus to

---

[4] Unesco, "World Heritage List," http://whc.unesco.org/en/list, accessed July 2012.
[5] US Census Bureau, "Total Ancestry reported," http://factfinder2.census.gov/faces/ tableservices/jsf/pages/productview.xhtml?pid=ACS_10_1YR_B04003&prodType=table, accessed July 2012.

the development of communicative competence. Intuitively, we all agree that in an L2 context the language is acquired faster and better. Many research studies confirm this perception.[6] Of particular benefit is pragmatic and intercultural competence as well as the understanding of the relationship between the practices and perspectives of cultural products.[7] Language-teaching approaches emphasize how language and culture go together, but in a foreign context this is more difficult to achieve. In an immersion course the student is constantly aware that they are the same thing, that language *is* culture.

Italy has one official language but there are also many *Italie*, many expressions and cultural products, differing from North to South. Italy is the home of many dialects, which are living organisms, used daily. They mingle and interact with standard Italian, enriching the vocabulary, modifying the pronunciation, and creating idioms. Only through immersion can students understand the richness of the sociolinguistic and sociocultural aspects of the Italian language.

Studying in Italy means not only studying Italian but also studying *in* Italian. Taking a course in History, Economics, Art, or Physics in Italian means learning the content, having access to new knowledge otherwise not practicable, it also means learning and improving language skills in an academic context, having access to other formal registers, different than those of daily interactions. Finally, Italy is constantly changing, no longer the land remembered by immigrants. It is important that the descendants of Italians in the U.S. know and understand the Italy of today, and not only the idealized one narrated to them by their grandparents or read about and seen depicted in the media.

Study in Italy

For college and high school students, there are many options to experience study abroad in Italy. They may participate in programs offered by international agencies, or through programs activated by their schools and colleges with Italian partners. Language courses or other subjects offered by many private schools throughout Italy offer yet another option. College and

---

[6] See Jiménez Jiménez 2010; Mohajeri Norris, Steinberg 2008; Duperron, Overstreet 2009 and references cited there, among others.
[7] See Dolci, Spinelli 2008; Doyle 2009, Rundstrom Williams 2009, and references cited there, among others.

university students could also attend one of the numerous branches of American universities in Italy, the so-called "*island*" programs, as they are sometimes labeled. In any case, one must be sure that the credits are recognized once back in the USA.

In Italy, according to the website of the U.S. Embassy, there are about 140 semester or year-abroad programs offered by accredited U.S. institutions of higher education and four degree-granting institutions as well as many international K-12 schools that offer courses in English and Italian.[8] There is also an association, named AACUPI (Association of American Colleges and Universities in Italy), which includes the American Colleges and Universities that have a program in Italy. There are campuses in 27 cities, large and small, scattered throughout Italy. They range from cities like Florence and Rome, respectively with 42 and 55 campuses and branches, to small towns like Asolo in Veneto or Alba in Piedmont.[9] There are also many private schools in all Italian regions that offer courses of varying duration ranging from language to cuisine. Some of these are grouped in an association, ASILS (Associazione delle Scuole d'Italiano come Lingua Seconda), created for the purpose of ensuring a high standard in the services offered.[10]

In Italy there are 81 universities that have about 800 agreements with American Colleges and Universities.[11] The agreements range from cooperation in research projects at the highest level, to the exchange of faculty and students and to the realization of joint degrees.[12]

Among the Italian universities most engaged in cooperation with the U.S. are the two Universities for Foreigners of Perugia and Siena, which, because of their role, are the most specialized in providing courses in Italian language and culture and offering degrees at the B.A., M.A., Ph.D., and professional M.A. levels.

---

[8] United States Diplomatic Mission to Italy, http://italy.usembassy.gov/reference/u.s.-education-in-italy.html, accessed July, 2012.
[9] Association of American College and University Programs in Italy, http://www.aacupi.org/home-frameset.htm, Accessed July 2012
[10] ASILS, http://www.asils.it/ accessed July 2012.
[11] Cineca, Accordi Internazionali Stati Uniti Italia, http://accordi-internazionali.cineca.it/ accordi.php?continenti=AM&paesi=840&univ_stran=%25&univ_ita=%25&anni=%25&btnSubmit=Cerca&pag=4, accessed July 2012.
[12] See also "Honors Center of Italian Universities," http://www.h2cu.com/, accessed July 2012.

The University for Foreigners of Perugia has research and exchange agreements with many American universities, and organizes courses of Italian language and culture for high school students, such as those who attend La Scuola d'Italia Guglielmo Marconi in New York. In addition, the University has launched specific agreements with the University of Maryland, Georgetown University, and CUNY Queens College at the MA level for the exchange of faculty and students in order to train future teachers and specialists.

The University for Foreigners of Perugia has always considered its relationship with the USA a fundamental one: it is one of the oldest, with the first agreement with an American institution of higher education, Smith College, dating back to 1931. The collaboration with the U.S. also involves associations such as The National Italian American Foundation (NIAF), which offers the winner of the "Teacher of the Year Award" a grant to study at the University for Foreigners of Perugia.

In 2010, the University for Foreigners opened an office at the John D. Calandra Italian American Institute, Queens College (CUNY) in New York (USA) for fostering the exchange of students and teachers with American Institutions. It has also established a foundation named "*Friends of the University for Foreigners of Perugia*", based in New York, whose main aim is to support the study of Italian language and culture in the U.S.

The support of Italian language is carried out not only through helping students, but also and especially through backing teachers. It is necessary to promote the training of qualified teachers, by offering more degrees that include specific education courses in the curriculum and encourage in-service training. This certainly will also reinforce the success of the Advanced Placement Program in Italian.

It is crucial for student teachers and in-service teachers to spend a period of study in Italy. In addition to the two specialized Universities for Foreigners, Perugia and Siena, many other universities offer training courses, Professional M.A. and teaching certifications.

An interesting project for the exchange of teachers has been activated between the Network of Autonomous Schools of the Lombardy Region and Dickinson College (Pennsylvania, USA), which coordinates the selection of assistants in 40 American universities under the auspices of the Italian Consulates in the U.S.[13]

Furthermore Italian-American organizations give a significant contribution to maintaining ties to Italy. Each organizes study and culture tours in Italy and offers scholarships for students and teachers both directly and through partnerships.

The Italian Embassy in Washington and its Consulates are constantly engaged in helping to find sponsors and funding. They also coordinate and provide scholarships through the institutions directly funded by the Ministry of Foreign Affairs. IACE (Italian American Committee on Education) is the largest in the United States and operates within the states of New York, Connecticut, and New Jersey. It organizes annual study trips to Italy. Also La Scuola Guglielmo Marconi of Italy in New York, the only one that offers the double American/Italian high school diploma in the U.S., has numerous exchanges with Italian schools.

The Observatory for the Italian Language in the United States, established by the Italian Embassy to monitor the development of AP Italian, has often emphasized the need to facilitate study travel in Italy. It has provided several scholarships for students preparing AP Italian and deserving to attend courses in Italy.

In conclusion, we can say that in order to study a language (and its culture) it is essential to study it where it is spoken. From the data available, it appears that students who study Italian have understood this better than others. If we compare the number of Italian students in colleges and universities in 2009 with the number of students who in the same year went to Italy to study, the ratio is 1 to 2,5. It is the highest one among the languages most studied abroad, as we have stressed earlier.

This is a good result, but there is still much to do, especially at the high school level. We have no reliable data for high schools, but we can assume that among the 78,213 students of Italian at K-12, of which approximately

---

[13] http://www.pacioli.net/it/index.php?option=com_content&task=view&id=193&Itemid=82: accessed, July 12.

80% range from grades 9-12 (IES 2011), there are at least a few thousand who studied in Italy for at least two weeks.

The promotion of study abroad in Italy is a difficult path, but the return on investment is certainly high and long lasting. The commitment of all stakeholders should be to remove as many obstacles as possible from the road. I would like to finish this contribution with the words of a student after her study abroad experience:

> Prima c'era l'euforia iniziale per la città, poi il disagio di un nuovo posto, e finalmente, ho assorbito tutta la cultura fantastica trovandoci comodità (e vi ho trovato conforto). L'esplorazione, il perdermi, vedere cose nuove, essere a disagio con le mie abilità di lingua, tutte sono state la migliore avventura. Queste esperienze aiutano a svilupparsi e migliorarsi come persone.[14]

Bibliography

Ambasciata d'Italia a Washington, "Cooperazione Economica," http://www.ambwashingtondc.esteri.it/Ambasciata_Washington/Menu/I_rapporti_bilaterali/Cooperazione_economica/ accessed, July 3, 2012.

Bolen, C. M. (ed.) *A Guide to Outcomes Assessment in Education Abroad*. Forum on Education Abroad, 2007.

Dolci, R. Spinelli, B., "Building an Intercultural Identity in a Cross-Cultural Transition: a Short Term Case Study," in Occhipinti E. (ed.) *Teaching Italian and Italian Culture: Case-Studies from an International Perspective*. Cambridge: Cambridge Scholars Publishing, 2008. 373-402.

Dolci, R., "Il *Quadro* e gli Standards for Foreign Language Learning," in Mezzadri M. (ed.), *Integrazione linguistica in Europa: Il Quadro comune di riferimento per le lingue*. Torino: Utet Libreria, 2006. 60-84.

Doyle, D. "Holistic Assessment and the Study Abroad Experience" *Frontiers*, Vol. XVIII (2009). 143-156.

Hayward, F. M., Siaya L. M., "Mapping Internationalization in US campuses," American Council on Education, 2003, http://www.acenet.edu/bookstore/pdf/mapping.pdf: retrieved, July 6 2012.

---

[14] Cited in Dolci, Spinelli 2008.

Hayward, F. M., Siaya L. M., "Report on Two National Surveys about International Education," American Council on Education, 2001, http://www.acenet.edu/bookstore/pdf/2001-intl-report.pdf: retrieved, July 15 2012.

IIE (Istitute of Interational Education), "Open doors. Report on International Educational Exchange 2011" http://www.iie.org/en/Research-and-Publications/Open-Doors: retrieved, July 3 2012.

Jimenez-Jimenez, A., "A Comparative Study on Second Language Vocabulary Development: Study Abroad vs. Classroom Settings," *Frontiers* XIX (2010): 105-124.

Mohajeri Norris, E., Steinberg, M., "Does Language Matter? The Impact of Language of Instruction on Study Abroad Outcomes," *Frontiers* XVII (2008): 107-131.

Norris, E. Gillespie, G. I., "How Study Abroad Shapes Global Careers Evidence From the United States," *Journal of Studies in International Education* 13.3 (2009): 382-397

Orahood, T., Kruze, L., Easley Pearson, D. "The Impact of Study Abroad on Business Students' Career Goals," *Frontiers* Vol. X (2004): 117-130

Pasternock, M. A., The American Student in Italy, *Italica* 33.4 (1956): 286-290

Rundstrom Williams, T., "The Reflective Model of Intercultural Competency: A Multidimensional, Qualitative Approach to Study Abroad Assessment," *Frontiers* XVIII (2009): 289-306

Santosuosso J. J. "ASTP characteristics in 55 colleges: 1941-1951," *Italica* 31.2 (1954): 99-105

Spolsky, B., *Language Policy*, Cambridge: Cambridge University Press, 2004

Sutton, R. C., Rubin, D. L., "Documenting the Academic Impact of Study Abroad: Final Report of the GLOSSARI Project". Paper presented at the NAFSA Annual Conference. Kansas City, Missouri, 4 June 2010, http://glossari.uga.edu/datasets/pdfs/FINAL.pdf: retrieved, 6 July 2012

Thompson, J. W., "An Exploration of the Demand for Study Overseas from American students and Employers" (no date), http://www.nafsa.org/_/File/_/study_by_iie_daad_bc.pdf: retrieved, 6 July 2012

Tilman, M., "Impact of Education abroad on Career Development, Vol. I," AIFS, 2005, http://www.aifsabroad.com/advisors/pdf/Impact_of_Education_AbroadI.pdf: retrieved, July 3 2005.

Trooboff, S., Van De Berg, M., Ryman J., "Employer Attitudes toward Study Abroad," *Frontiers* XV (2008): 17-34

Wright, S., *Language Policy and Language Planning*. New York: Palgrave MacMillan, 2004

Useful Links

A.S.I.L.S., Associazione delle scuole di italiano come lingua seconda: http://www.asils.it/

Accordi Internazionali Universitari Stati Uniti-Italia, http://accordi-internazionali.cineca.it/accordi.php?continenti=AM&paesi=840&univ_stran=%25&univ_ita=%25&anni=%25&btnSubmit=Cerca&pag=4,

Ambasciata Italiana a Washington http://www.ambwashingtondc.esteri.it/Ambasciata_Washington

Association of American College and University Programs in Italy, http://www.aacupi.org/home-frameset.htm,

H2CU Honors center of Italian Universities: http://www.h2cu.com/

MAE (Ministero degli Affari Esteri): http://www.esteri.it/MAE/IT/Ministero/Servizi/Stranieri/Opportunita/BorseStudio_stranieri.htm

MIUR (Ministero dell'Univerістà e della Ricerca): http://www.universitaly.it/

MIUR (Ministero dell'Università e della Ricerca), Italian Higher Education for Foreign Students: http://www.study-in-italy.it/

Observatory for the Italian Language in the USA: http://www.usspeaksitalian.org/

United States Diplomatic Mission to Italy: http://italy.usembassy.gov/reference/u.s.-education-in-italy.html

Università per Stranieri di Perugia: www.unistrapg.it

Università per Stranieri di Siena: www.unistrasi.it

US-Italy Fulbright Commission: http://www.fulbright.it/en

Learning from the Medicis
Patronage at Work

Professor Anthony Julian Tamburri
John D. Calandra Italian American Institute
Queens College, CUNY

On December 5, 2010, I sent out a message entitled "From the Dean's Desk" through the John D. Calandra Italian American Institute's listserve. It was in reaction to a *New York Times* article that appeared that very day and spoke to the precarious state of affairs for western European languages.[1] The article appeared in the wake of the success of re-instating the College Board's Advanced Placement Program in Italian.

It was a bit like a pail of cold water being thrown at us for a number of reasons: first, we had just come off of the successful campaign of getting the Advanced Placement Program in Italian re-instated; second, the threatening of Italian in particular remains most peculiar since there has been a constant increase in students studying Italian since 1969, when numbers were first registered (approx. 700% in these past forty-one years).

Italian continues to be one of the few languages registering growth, which makes the struggle to save programs and the re-instatement of the Advanced Placement Program in Italian (AP) all the more significant. We have come to realize, I would submit to you, that these past three years (the College Board threatened the eventual suspension of the AP in Italian in January 2008) have proven that only by collaborating as a community at large can we achieve any sort of success. Such re-instatement of the AP did in fact challenge the various Italian/American communities to raise three million dollars that would finance the future of the exam.[2]

That 2009 campaign was initially coordinated and led by the Conference

---

[1] See Lisa Foderaro's article "Budget-Cutting Colleges Bid Some Languages Adieu" (http://www.nytimes.com/2010/12/05/education/05languages.html?ref=languageandlanguages).
[2] For the past two decades I have opted for the slash ("/") over the hyphen ("-"). For more on this, see my *To Hyphenate or Not to Hyphenate. The Italian/American Writer: Or, An Other American?* (Montréal: Guernica, 1991).

of Presidents of Major Italian American Organizations (COP). The leadership of the COP, it is important to underscore, was instrumental in getting negotiations back on track in early 2009. That leadership partnered with the American Society for the Italian Legions of Merit (ASILM), who together formed a working committee that helped re-launch talks with the College Board in September 2009. In October 2009, Giulio Terzi di Sant'Agata was named Italy's new Ambassador to the United States; and he immediately embraced the cause to re-instate the AP in Italian. I mention this only because, as a community, we need to know who all the so-called brokers were and, when we cross paths, thank them all for their *impegno* (commitment). The other organizations that fundraised and assisted in significant ways included, in alphabetical order, the American Association of Teachers of Italian (AATI), the Columbus Citizens Foundation, the Italian Consulate of New York and the Italian Embassy in DC, the Italian Heritage and Culture Committee of New York, Italian Language Foundation (ILF), Italian Language Inter-Culture Alliance (ILICA), National Italian American Foundation (NIAF), National Organization of Italian American Women (NOIAW), Order Sons of Italy in America (OSIA), representatives of the University of Perugia for Foreigners, and others as well who individually contributed.[3]

Two days later, another article appeared on *The World*'s website (http://www.theworld.org/2010/12/07/italian-language-learning-in-america): "Is Italian finito in America." While the article is basically about the latest Italian food establishment in Manhattan, Eataly, it references the cultural tragedy of SUNY Albany. In so doing, the journalist writes:

> The survival of a language in schools and colleges is mostly about money. It's also about confidence. If students can't be sure schools are committed to a language, they'll be unlikely to commit to it themselves. Still, Italian's not in danger of disappearing from American education. Almost 80 thousand high schoolers took the language in 2007/8, the most recent figures available. And don't forget, not all learners are in formal education.

---

[3] Here, we would be remiss not to acknowledge Hon. Frank Guarini's invaluable commitment of $250,000 to the fund to re-instate the AP in Italian. On an institutional level, the Italian Embassy to the United States raised $1,500,000, while NIAF and the Columbus Citizen's Foundation contributed $500,000 each. The rest of the monies was generously provided by the institutions mentioned above as well as the current president of the Italian American Committee on Education, Berardo Paradiso.

What is stated above is true, the "survival of [Italian] is mostly about money," whether we like it or not. One reason for this may very well be that because, in the past, we as a community have not zeroed in on the language issue. Regardless of whether one speaks the language, s/he can always be a promoter of that language, if for any other reason than to be sure that those who follow do not suffer the consequences of "enemy alien" status when people in the United States (read also, young Italians), for example, were told not to speak the "enemy's language."[4] And as a consequence, this form of Americanization of an entire generation of children and grandchildren of all immigrants sent one of the most damaging and patently xenophobic messages it could have to the progeny of all of those who risked their lives to cross the ocean at the turn of the twentieth century.

It was a message sent out to non-Italians as well. Italian was no longer a good language to know; it was the "enemy's language"; it was the language of immigrants; it was also good for getting a good seat in an Italian restaurant, or for dealing with bootleggers, as Luigi Barzini, Jr. writes in his autobiography (*O America, When You and I Were Young*), when he recounts his American girl-friend's mother's little speech to him before they set foot on land in New York:

> "Luigi," her mother asked in a mellifluous voice, "you like Natalie?" I merely nodded enthusiastically but respectfully, as I could not speak. "Natalie likes you?" she went on. I modestly adopted a questioning look and waited. "I hope you speak Italian with her sometimes. She must get some practice. *Italian is very useful in New York, don't you know, particularly with bootleggers and headwaiters in good restaurants. They give you a better table if you speak their language.* They say that some people who know Italian can even understand the words of an opera and follow the plot, not

---

[4] For a chronology of governmental documentation, see the following website: http://italian.about.com/gi/dynamic/offsite.htm?site=http://www.foitimes.com/internment/chrono.html. For more on the history of this unspoken event, see *Alien Justice: Wartime Internment in Australia and North America*, Kay Saunders and Roger Daniels, eds. (St. Lucia, Qld.: University of Queensland Press, 2000); Lawrence DiStasi, editor, *Una Storia Segreta: The Secret History of Italian American Evacuation and Internment During World War II* (Berkeley, CA: Heyday Books, 2001) and Steven R. Fox, *UnCivil Liberties: Italian Americans Under Siege during World War II* (Boca Raton: Universal Publishers, 2000 [1990]).

that that makes much difference...." I found the strength to assure her I often spoke Italian with Natalie. I promised I would speak more, although it was more vital for me to fortify my English.

She continued: "I love your language. I don't understand it, but it is so musical. It is the language of love.... There's nothing more charming than a shipboard flirtation like yours. You're only young once, I always say. But there is one thing I must absolutely tell you. When we're in New York, do not try to see Natalie again. She has plenty of beaux. You won't like it. *And my husband, her father, disapproves of Italians. He dislikes having them around the house. They make him nervous. Italians, he says, are all right in Italy but even there he thinks there are far too many of them.* So promise me not to call or write. You understand, don't you?"[5]

Italian was, basically speaking, considered an ethnic language, for sure – good even, as "[t]hey say," to "understand the words of an opera and follow the plot, not that that makes much difference." It was a language for fun, to provide one with "divertimento," as we might ambiguously state in Italian: entertainment on the one hand, and diversion on the other. But, in the end, it was a language of people who "make [others] nervous" and who are, in addition, *"far too many."* This, of course, we know to be patently false! Italian is, to be sure, a language of culture, of world culture, and we must underscore this message whenever possible.

Our responsibility at this juncture is thus to ensure that the value of Italian is more than an ethnic language, more useful than for getting good seats in restaurants. Precisely because of the value of our Italian legacy, we need to be sure that Italian is available to all those who wish to study it. One thing we do know is that enrollments in Italian have increased significantly in these past twenty years.

We need to invest the same energies in this new campaign of not only saving Italian courses and programs, as we are being told today in the media. But we need to be better informed citizens of Italian America and more knowledgeable about our culture so that we can make the convincing argument that Italian should indeed be taught because of its more than 800 years

---

[5] Luigi Barzini, Jr., *O America, When You and I Were Young* (New York: Harper & Row, 1977) 135-6; my emphasis.

of culture, philosophy, science, and the arts. And the success of such actions lies squarely with us, both the Italian/American community and all those who love things Italian. We need to support our own activities, which means attending lectures that, in the end, truly do lead us toward a greater completeness of knowledge of our culture. We need to respond with courteous yet firm indignation when – whether it be at a social event or business meeting – someone makes an offensive comment about Italians or Italian Americans in his/her feeble attempt to make a joke.

We also need to do so for the teaching of Italian language and culture; we need to hold workshops around the country in order to hone further the quality of our teaching of the language, a job we have obviously been doing very well given the dramatic increases in enrollments over the years. This further investigation into different and more productive measures for teaching Italian is exactly what The Joseph and Elda Coccia Institute for the Italian Experience in America embarked upon with the inaugural "Teaching Italian Symposium. Meeting I: Speaking" of 2008.[6] While the workshop was aimed primarily at teachers from New Jersey, the Institute had gathered a national team of internationally renowned teachers of Italian language and culture. They explored teaching oral skills through a variety of ways that included various exercises students could perform individually to how they can work in a group, to how they can work with various media.

The 2009 edition of the symposium was dedicated to writing ("Teaching Italian Symposium. Meeting II: Writing"). Here, too, the Institute gathered an equally impressive team of leaders, both local and national, who worked with teachers from the tri-state area. Indeed, this type of synergy is emblematic of what we should be doing on a greater scale, working together and collaborating for the realization of the final goal, in this case the delivery of a subject matter in its most productive channels possible. This is, in fact, what we did as a community for the reinstatement of the AP in Italian; we worked as a team.

The 2010 symposium, "Teaching Italian Symposium. Meeting III: 'Technology,' 'Getting with the Program'," raised the bar even higher. In addressing additional needs for enhancing further still the teaching (and thus

---

[6] For more on the Coccia Institute and the Coccia Foundation, see their respective websites at the following urls: http://chss.montclair.edu/cocciainstitute and http://www.cocciafoundation.org.

learning) of Italian, this workshop proved to be more broad-reaching than before, building nicely indeed on the previous two workshops. In this third year, we found an even greater interest in who wanted to attend the workshop. No longer just the locals, but indeed people coming from beyond the tri-state area. And this should be, for sure, one of our goals – to create an even greater network of professional competencies in language teaching.

This third year also inaugurated the Coccia-Inserra Award for Excellence and Innovation in the Teaching of Italian (K–12). This inaugural award went to Rina Miraglia, an Italian teacher at Ho-Ho-Kus Public School. The $1,000 prize was to be used to advance its Italian language and culture curriculum and programming. For this we need to thank both Cav. Joseph Coccia, Jr. and Lawrence R. Inserra, Jr., who have clearly exhibited their awareness of the necessity of both recognizing and supporting, in the Renaissance notion of patronage, the teaching of Italian language and culture.[7]

In a complementary path, ILICA, the Italian Language Inter-Cultural Alliance, has engaged in a similar type of philanthropy, geared in particular more toward the cultural. Founded in 2003, ILICA has had a conspicuous presence at both the ACTFL and NECTFL conferences as a major sponsor of their "Viale Italia" for a number of years. More in tune with its basic mission, ILICA has organized an annual cultural event that has either commemorated an anniversary (e.g., "Gli italiani cent'anni dopo [2005]) or investigated more current issues immediate to those both in Italy and in the United States (e.g., CHIASMI, a meeting of doctoral students of Brown and Harvard [2009]), be they Italian or non Italian alike. Indeed, its mission is very much in tune with an ecumenical spirit that calls all to the proverbial table; on its website, in fact, we read that it is "dedicated to the promotion of the Italian language as an instrument of understanding and study of a culture in continuous evolution, directed at Americans of Italian origin, and all those ethnic groups that share interest in learning the Italian language as a key to understanding

---

[7] In a similar manner the American Association of Teachers of Italian has engaged in similar activities these past two years, in its efforts to bolster the teaching of Italian at the advanced levels in high schools, with a particular emphasis on methodologies for teaching Advanced Placement courses in Italian. Various workshops in this regard have been held throughout the east coast as of this writing. They have ranged from the Northeast to the Southeast; form Boston to Miami; and further workshops are in the planning for the Midwest and the West.

Italian culture within the context of the 21st century."⁸ Language and culture are intertwined, the former being the key to a greater access to the latter, something that was apparently lost on the likes of a Richard Haass or John McWhorter.⁹

Three of ILICA's more recent activities underscore this emphasis on the cultural, with a much broader scope of who might be its audience, than what seems to be the proverbial Italian/American community. In 2009, embracing a theme so large as that of environmental sustainability, ILICA organized an international conference entitled "The MOSE Project 'Saving Venezia and protecting New Orleans'." This was an all-day conference with experts from Venice and New Orleans each of whom offered opposing positions on how to save these two cities. Italian and American positions were juxtaposed side by side in a bilingual forum.

In 2011, in turn, ILICA organized yet another of it's all-day conferences. This one, in tune with the theme of the year, the 150th anniversary of Italy's unification, was dedicated to Italy's age-old *questione meridionale*, the Southern Question. The event was organized around a conversation with the authors of two best sellers in Italy, Pino Aprile's *Terroni* and Lorenzo Del Boca's *Polentoni*;¹⁰ two other speakers accompanied each author, all of which was moderated by yet a seventh person. With the assistance of simultaneous

---

⁸ More detailed information on ILICA's many activities and sponsorships can be found on its website at: http://www.ilicait.org.
⁹ President of a think-tank, Council on Foreign Relations, Richard N. Haass was the invited key-note speaker at the 2010 annual conference of the American Council on the Teaching of Foreign Languages. In that speech, he challenged the prominence of European language instruction, mentioning specifically Italian, with relationship to locales of political agitation in places all over the world. Of course, one might indeed muse about the choice of speaker. But that is for another venue.
In a similar vein, John McWhorter also downplayed knowledge of western-European languages in his *The New Republic* blog of December 13 2010 (http://www.tnr.com/blog/john-mcwhorter/79843/which-languages-should-liberal-arts-be-about-in-2010). There, he told us that he did not feel as bad about "this new trend [i.e., "the disappearance of French, German, and Italian departments"] as [he is] supposed to," despite the fact that he is a "former French major and great fan of foreign language learning." It is, in fact, his use of the word "trend" that I found both problematic and, I would underscore, emblematic of a certain dominant cultural trait in the United States vis-à-vis languages other than English. See my response on i-Italy.org (http://www.i-italy.org/bloggers/17595/why-liberal-arts-should-be-about-all-languages).
¹⁰ Pino Aprile, *Terroni. Tutto quello che è stato fatto perché gli italiani del sud diventassero "Meridionali* (Milan: Piemme, 2010), and Lorenzo Del Boca, *Polentoni. Come e perché il Nord è stato tradito* (Milan: Piemme, 2011). In another act of philanthropy/patronage, ILICA also funded the translation into English of Aprile's *Terroni* and Del Boca's *Polentoni*, published by Bordighera Press.

translation, the conversation itself lasted close to three hours of various exchanges that included different perspectives of how Italy was unified and who/which side may have benefitted the most. Lively, respectful, and most informative, the attendees came away with a reserve of information not previously available to such an audience in the United States.

Finally, in 2012, ILICA hosted a two-day symposium, "On a Different Shore: Defining Italian, Italian Identity in the Third Millennium." Dedicated to exploring notions of "Italian" (read, also, Italian/American) identity, ILICA gathered four people from Italy and four from the Italian/American community. The conversation began one afternoon at Queens College (CUNY) and continued a second afternoon at John Jay College (CUNY). The conversation was fruitful and productive, as the eight speakers dealt with issues of identity that were seen from two different perspectives, Italian and Italian/American. The conclusion was that a follow-up is necessary in order to continue the conversation.[11]

Both forms of linguistic and cultural support that the Coccia Foundation and ILICA have provided thus far over the years constitute a basic form of philanthropy that, most would readily agree, has its roots in that form of Renaissance patronage that was so readily practiced by the Medici's especially in the second half of the fifteenth century. Patronage, in fact, is at the base of the Coccia Foundation's The Amici Student Groups, that, as we read on the Foundation's website, is "a growing network of Italian clubs, representing numerous colleges and universities around the country, who have the opportunity to communicate and coordinate with each other through the Coccia Foundation."

Patronage also clearly subtends those activities sponsored by ILICA. In addition to what we have mentioned above, ILICA has also organized and funded other symposia in Italy and in the United States on a variety of topics that have also had at their base Italian as the underlying theme: "L'Italiano Da Ponte tra l'Italia e gli Stati Uniti" ("The Italian Da Ponte between Italy and the USA"; 2006); "Italia USA – Lingua, Cultura, Identità" ("Italy USA – Language, Culture, Identity"; 2010); "Italia USA – Italiano, Impresa, Innovazione" ("Italy USA – Italian, Business, Innovation"; 2011).

---

[11] One day before the symposium, ILICA sponsored a discussion on the current economic situation in Italy and what the future promises.

All of the above constitute both patronage and network-making in one stroke, so to speak. Both the Coccia Institute and ILICA have clearly looked back to that wonderful practice that was Renaissance patronage and brought it into the twenty-first century. In so doing, they have helped in the creation of a synergy, on the one hand, at the national level among college students with a passion for all things Italian, and, on the other, at the international level, an invaluable collaboration of scholars and entrepreneurs.

All of these actions and collaborations mentioned above is what we need to expand, from the local to the global. And The Joseph and Elda Coccia Institute for the Italian Experience in America at Montclair State University and ILICA, the Italian Language Inter-Cultural Alliance, have offered what can only be excellent models to emulate. Only in this sense can we engage in a more productive and greater degree of a cultural and ethnic discourse, one that clearly surpasses those ethnic boundaries of social events; it is simply not enough for any of us, private or elected individuals, to proclaim our Italian pride at Italian events. We need to do so at events and in venues that are *not* Italian and Italian/American. We need to uphold the value of our Italian heritage and legacy in its various and multifaceted manifestations and articulations in these venues precisely because, for instance, (1) what we know today as "modernity" has its origins in the Italian Renaissance; (2) what we know as "philanthropy" today has its roots in the Italian Renaissance practice of patronage; (3) what we know today as the United States legal system, it has its roots in an eighteenth-century Italian legal philosopher, Cesare Beccaria; (4) what we know of the art world today is that more than sixty-percent of the world's production is Italian in origin; (5) what we know of United States contemporary literature is that some of our best-selling authors are David Baldacci, Rita Ciresi, Don DeLillo, Lisa Scottoline, and Adriana Trigiani, to name a few.

Here at the Calandra Institute (Queens College, CUNY), we have and shall continue to partner with all of the associations and organizations mentioned at the outset. Together with them – with both The Joseph and Elda Coccia Institute for the Italian Experience in America and ILICA, in organizational collaborations in particular – will we be able to insure that Italian and Italian/American history and culture, as well as the Italian language, do not fall by the wayside because of decisions made by bureaucrats and functionaries grounded only in what they perceive as the latest notions of what is solely "utilitarian" when it comes to the knowledge and linguistic competency of a second language and the culture that it represents.

ITALIAN
A GATEWAY TO EUROPE, A BRIDGE TO THE FUTURE

Claudio Bisogniero
Italian Ambassador to the United States

"More Italian in the USA," in other words, promoting Italian in the United States through our consular network and cultural institutes, is one of our core "mission statements."

Italy and the United States have long enjoyed strong bonds of friendship, based on our common values and shared ideals, and I firmly believe that they can be enhanced through the diffusion of Italian language and culture in the United States. I am not alone in this belief: indeed, the Italian President of the Republic, the Prime Minister, and the Minister of Foreign Affairs have all noted how important it is to promote our language in this great country.

My Government has spared no efforts in supporting this campaign, and it has worked closely with the Conference of Presidents of Major Italian American Organizations and with prominent Italian groups and companies. Through these joint efforts we have been able to attain notable goals, such as reinstating Italian in the AP Program (November 2010), a critical step in ensuring the teaching of our language at the high school and university level.

During his visit to New York for the 150th Anniversary of Italy's Unification, President Giorgio Napolitano underlined the formative role that Italian played in the building of our country. In his words, Italian was a "founding moment of national identity" and "one of the most ancient and noble cultural forces that have united our country and kept our citizens together and cohesive abroad."

The 14th-century idiom of Dante, Petrarch, and Boccaccio is perfectly comprehensible to this day, and was fundamental in shaping the cultural unity of our country. Tradition and innovation enabled it to evolve and become the *lingua franca* of a country that was marked by many different vernaculars: indeed, Italy was *one* from a linguistic point of view long before it became a unified State. So, while our language has remained true to its origins, it has also proved its versatility by adapting to changing times. Not many other modern languages can say the same, and Italian is second to none in its ability to evolve and transform and yet retain its originality.

We can certainly say that our culture has found its match in our language! In fact, this year, 2013, is the "Year of Italian Culture in the United States." Throughout the year we will showcase Italian culture with a high profile program of events in cities throughout the United States. Italy's areas of excellence – the visual arts, music, food, fashion and design along with discovery and research – will be presented and promoted in all of their many different and exciting facets throughout the year. The common thread behind the year is – yes, you've guessed it! – precisely that creativity, that ability to join tradition and innovation that is one of our country's most distinctive hallmarks. And in America, a country renowned for welcoming the free flow of ideas, this Italian talent finds fertile ground for advancement and development.

We must not forget that Italian wielded – and continues to wield – great influence on other European and Mediterranean languages, in so many different domains – be it mathematics, maritime sciences, banking, music, poetry, the visual arts, food, and fashion. Where would we be today without "bravo," "maestro," "allegro" and "crescendo," or "al dente," "espresso," or yet "chiaroscuro," "replica" and "terracotta," not to mention "scenario," "manifesto" and "propaganda" to name but a few? Indeed, America owes its very name to an Italian!

Yet the role of our language does not stop here. Indeed, mirroring Italy's own capacity as a formidable cultural and political mediator, over the centuries it developed an extraordinary ability to act as a bridge between the different communities along the Mediterranean. For example, through it many Arabic words have migrated to other European languages.

Walt Whitman, one of the masters of American literature, once said this of the United States: "I am big. I contain multitudes." As my predecessor, now Italian Minister of Foreign Affairs Giulio Terzi, remarked at the Annual AP Conference in San Francisco in July 2011, this is also the secret to the greatness of Italian culture and language: it contains multitudes. It brings closer, it integrates, it binds: this is one of the Italian language's most distinctive features. And how could it be any different, when it reflects the history of the greatest cultural and humanistic reality in the world? A country that, according to UNESCO, is home to over half of the world's artistic and cultural heritage.

In modern times, this "bridging" role has been embraced by the millions of Italians who have moved abroad to all continents. This is particularly true for the Italian and Italian-American communities in the United States. President Obama expressly recalled, both in his Proclamation for the 150th Anniversary of the Unification of Italy, and in the October 2011 NIAF Gala dinner, our community's extraordinary contribution to this Country.

It is they who have helped to shape the very foundations of the United States. The "unalienable rights" cited in the Declaration of Independence – notably life, liberty, and the pursuit of happiness – derive from the concept of the "centrality of the human being" which was so crucial to the thinking of the Renaissance. Filippo Mazzei and Thomas Jefferson enjoyed a great friendship: the "All men are equal" phrase enshrined in the "Declaration of Independence" is attributed to the Italian philosopher.

Gaetano Filangieri and Benjamin Franklin also had a long and productive correspondence, which brought together the former's dream of a universal constitution with the solid strength of a nascent federal State. A country where freedom and equality could finally be achieved.

As for the pursuit of happiness, it's easy to see how it connects to what today is referred to as the "Italian style" – a concept that encompasses much broader ideas, such as the Mediterranean diet and healthy living, which today is a priority for all governments.

Italian is now the fourth most studied foreign language in the United States. In California, according to recent figures, it has become the third.

After reinstating AP Italian, we launched a campaign to enhance the appeal of our language at all levels. In this, the Observatory of the Italian Language, which works with representatives of donor organizations, teacher associations, university professors, and high-school teachers, and directs all activities pertaining to the dissemination of the Italian language in the United States, plays a crucial role. Its strategic plan was approved by the College Board, and it works closely with our Institutes of Culture and with structures of excellence such as "La Scuola d'Italia Guglielmo Marconi" in New York.

The Observatory has distributed grants to teachers for seminars and training courses in cooperation with prestigious institutions such as AATI, ACTFL, and Middlebury College. It has also printed and widely distributed literature on the importance and advantages of studying Italian, and has launched its own website, www.usspeaksitalian.org.

Last but not least, I must note the important role of the many interuniversity agreements between Italian and American institutions – such as that one signed by the University of Maryland and the University for Foreigners of Perugia, which will promote a new generation of Italian language teachers. Or again, by the Memoranda of Understanding that exist at a State, County, or School District level.

As we look ahead to the Year of Italian Culture in the United States, we must not forget the over 700 cooperation agreements in science, research and innovation between American and Italian universities in the most diverse and dynamic scientific matters. Through these, and the exchange programs for researchers, American scholars and students are able to touch some of Italy's areas of excellence – such as technology and innovation – first hand.

And this – together with the increasing economic and trade cooperation between our two nations, and the immense business opportunities this entails – provides, as if there was any need for one, yet another reason and incentive – perhaps an excuse?! – to study Italian.

Let the US speak Italian. Let us all speak Italian!

Contributors

LIDIA MATTICCHIO BASTIANICH is one of the most-loved chefs on television, a best-selling cookbook author, and restaurateur. She has held true to her Italian roots and culture, which she proudly and warmly invites her fans to experience. She is the author of nine cookbooks, the latest *Lidia's Favorite Recipes: 100 Foolproof Dishes, from the Basic Sauces to Irresistible Entrées*, which she co-authored with Tanya Biastianich Manuali. Some other titles are: *Lidia's Italy in America*; *Lidia Cooks from the Heart of Italy*; *Lidia's Family Table*; and *Lidia's Italian-American Kitchen*. Five of her books were accompanied by nationally syndicated public television series. She is the owner of the New York City restaurant Felida, as well as co-ownership in other restaurants in New York City, which include Becco, Del Posto, and Eataly. In addition to being a prolific author, chef, and restaurateur, she also lectures regularly across the country on Italian cuisine. In like fashion, since 1998 she has been a regular on PBS television with her own show and numerous specials. In January 2013, Chef Lidia Matticchio Bastianich was inducted into the Culinary Hall of Fame.

CLAUDIO BISOGNIERO is the Ambassador of Italy to the United States. Born in Rome, he earned a Degree in Political Science from the University of Rome (1976) with a dissertation in International Economics. He entered the Italian Foreign Service in May 1978. Before arriving as Italy's Ambassador to the United States, Bisogniero has held numerous diplomatic posts throughout his career, beginning in China, then to Brussels, New York, Rome, covering various duties at different agencies including the IMF and World Bank, the United Nations, NATO, and the G8. In October 2007, he took up his duties as NATO Deputy Secretary General, responsible for a variety of security and strategic issues on the Alliance's agenda; he also followed the NATO Summits in Bucharest, Strasbourg/Kiel, and Lisbon, and worked actively in the preparatory phase for the 2012 NATO Summit in Chicago. He has been Ambassador of Italy to the United States since January 18, 2012. Claudio Bisogniero is married to Laura Denise Noce Benigni Olivieri; they have a daughter and a son.

ROBERTO DOLCI is Associate Professor of Applied and Educational Linguistics at the Università per Stranieri di Perugia, Italy, where he is also the Scientific Director of the Italian Language Courses for Erasmus Students, and the Scientific Director of the National Research Project on "Lingua Italiana in Rete per l'Apprendimento." He has published widely on educational technology, intercultural competence, and

Language Education Policy. He is also a visiting scholar at the John D. Calandra Institute, Queens College/CUNY, where he also teaches on language pedagogy.

CLORINDA DONATO is the George L. Graziadio Chair of Italian Studies at California State University, Long Beach and Professor of French and Italian. She has also been recognized as *Chevalier dans l'Ordre des Palmes Académiques*. In the area of second-language acquisition, she is working on French and Italian for Spanish Speakers, and is the Principal Investigator for a three-year NEH grant on this topic. Encyclopedism, Italian-Swiss relations, and European enlightenments are the subject of numerous publications, among them three co-edited volumes. *Jesuit Accounts of the Colonial Americas—Textualities, Intellectual Disputes, Intercultural Transfers* is forthcoming in 2013 with the University of Toronto Press in the UCLA Clark Library publication series.

HERMANN HALLER is Professor of Italian at Queens College and Professor of Comparative Literature and French at the Graduate Center, The City University of New York. He is the author of *Una lingua perduta e ritrovata: l'italiano degli italo-americani* (1993), *The Other Italy. The literary canon in dialect* (1999), *La festa delle lingue. La letteratura dialettale in Italia* (2002), *Tra Napoli e New York. Le macchiette italo-americane di Eduardo Migliaccio* (2006). He has also authored numerous articles published in European and American scholarly journals. He was Visiting Professor at Johns Hopkins University, at the University of Pennsylvania, and at the Universities of Florence, Genoa, Trent, and Milan. He is a past president of the International Linguistic Association and a member of the Accademia della Crusca (Socio corrispondente straniero).

FRED GARDAPHÉ is Distinguished Professor of English and Italian American Studies at Queens College and the John D. Calandra Italian American Institute, of the City University of New York. He directs the Italian American Studies Program at Queens College. He is past director of Stony Brook University's American and Italian/American Studies programs. His books include *Italian Signs, American Streets: The Evolution of Italian American Narrative*; *Dagoes Read: Tradition and the Italian/American Writer*; *Moustache Pete is Dead!*; *Leaving Little Italy*; and *From Wiseguys to Wise Men: Masculinities and the Italian American Gangster*; and *The Art of Reading Italian Americana*. His most recent book, *Segni italiani, strade americane: l'evoluzione della letteratura italiana americana*, is the translation of his *Italian Signs, American Streets* and was published in Italy in 2012. He is co-founding/co-editor of *VIA: Voices in Italian Americana* and editor of the Italian American Culture Series of SUNY Press. He is an editor of I-Italy.org and of H-ITAM.

Grand'Ufficiale SILVANA MANGIONE, Juris Doctor from the University of Bologna, Italy, is the Deputy Secretary General of the General Council of Italians Abroad, an international body chaired by the Italian Minister of Foreign Affairs. She is the Editorial Director of Idea Publications, a small publishing house committed to "cultura di ritorno," a cultural recognition between Italians residing at the two sides of the Atlantic, and a member of the Executive Committee of IACE – Italian American Committee on Education. Public relations consultant for Italian governmental and private entities, journalist, translator and writer, she has taught courses, written articles and lectured extensively on Italian emigration, Italian law, history, politics, and women's rights. She also holds a Diploma in Drama from the Antoniano of Bologna and has worked as opera director in Italy, and liaison between Teatro alla Scala of Milan and the Kennedy Center and the Metropolitan Opera of New York, as well as teaching theater courses for children at the Smithsonian Institution and Master classes in acting and pronunciation for opera singers. With the John D. Calandra Italian American Institute (Queens College, CUNY), she has helped organize two Symposia on the poet/trade unionist Arturo Giovannitti and celebrate the centennial of his famous self-defense in Salem, Massachusetts.

VINCENZO MARRA is the President and Founder of ILICA, the Italian Language Inter-Cultural Alliance. His numerous contributions to the Italian American community prompted him to be recognized by many organizations, including the Italian government. Vincenzo was a member of the Board of Directors of NIAF and served as Regional Vice President for New York. He also acted as Advisor to the Chairman for over twenty years. He is listed in the Italian book *Italiani nel mondo* and is listed in *Who's Who Among Italian Americans*. Marra has been President of Assisi Pax International and has served as the Manhattan Chapter President of Legatus, the International Organization for "Selected Catholic Business Leaders". Marra was also the first Ambassador of OSIA (Order Sons of Italy in America). He was honored by the NYPD's Columbia Association as Business Entrepreneur of the Year and received the FDNY's Humanitarian of the Year Award as well. He has been Man of the Year for NOIAW (National Organization of Italian American Women), the Children's Skin Disease Foundation, the Italian Welfare League, and the National Council of Columbia Associations in Civil Services. Cav. Marra also received the Italian Ministry of Foreign Affairs Medal for Italians Abroad from Minister Mirko Tremaglia. Cav. Marra is a Knight of the Order of Merit of the Italian Republic.

BERARDO PARADISO was born (Buonalbergo, Benevento), raised, and educated in Italy. He has a degree in mechanical engineering from the University of Naples, Italy. Fluent in several languages (Italian, English, French, and Spanish), Paradiso has a truly international work experience. From 1975-78 he worked as Production Manager of Guex Switzerland in Nyon, Switzerland; from 1978-81 he was President of Philippe Guex Tooling & Fastening in Puerto Rico; from 1981-87 he was Vice President of Allied Specialty in New York; and from 1987 to the present President of International Tool Mfg. in New York, which he founded. Paradiso belongs to many professional organizations, which include: President of IACE (Italian American Committee on Education); former President of the Italy America Chamber of Commerce in New York; Delegate and Board Member of the Accademia Italiana della Cucina, New York Soho; Board of Directors of the Dicapo Opera House in New York; former Chairman of the 10 Italian Chambers of Commerce in the NAFTA area; Board of Directors of the ASILM (The American Society of the Italian Legions of Merit); Board of Directors of the Italian Culture Month in NY. He writes on economic issues and cultural issues as guest writer for numerous Italian magazines. He resides in Great Neck, N.Y. with his wife Loyse. They have two children: Alberic, a graduate of NYU and Columbia, and Aurelie, an architect with degrees from Columbia and Yale.

EUGENIA PAULICELLI Professor of Italian, Comparative Literature and Women's Studies at Queens College and the Graduate Center, where she is also appointed in the Master of Arts in Liberal Studies (MALS) and coordinates Fashion Studies in Interdisciplinary Studies and in MALS. She has published widely on the history and theory of fashion. Her books include, *Fashion under Fascism. Beyond the Black Shirt* (Berg, 2004); *Moda e Moderno dal Medioevo al Rinascimento*, ed. (Meltemi, 2006); co-editor, *The Fabric of Cultures. Fashion, Identity, Globalization* (Routledge: 2009); co-editor, *1960. Un anno in Italia, Costume, Cinema, Moda e Cultura* (Il Ponte Vecchio, 2010); *The Fictions of Fashion in Early Modern Italy. From Sprezzatura to Satire* (Ashgate, forthcoming); *Italian Style. Fashion and Film 1914 to the Present* (Continuum Press, forthcoming). She is also guest editor of an issue of *Women's Studies Quarterly* dedicated to fashion (CUNY Feminist Press, 2013); and guest editor of an issue of the *Journal of Modern Italian Studies* entitled *Italian Fashion: Yesterday, Today and Tomorrow* (Spring, 2014).

NATALIA QUINTAVALLE is a career diplomat with 25 years of experience. In the past ten years, she has worked on UN issues, first at the Italian Permanent Mission in Geneva, where she was in charge of the relations with UN specialized agencies, including WHO and ILO, and then at the Permanent Mission in New York, where she represented Italy in the GA Fifth Committee and was subsequently in charge of the economic and development office. She served until September 2011 as Deputy Director General for political affairs and Principal Director for United Nations and Human Rights. Between 1986 and 1999, she served twice (1986-1988 and 1997-1999) at the General Directorate for Development Cooperation. She was appointed as Italian Consul in Toulouse, France (1989-1991) and as First Secretary at the Italian Embassy in Riyadh Saudi Arabia, (1991-1995). She has been appointed as Italian Consul General in New York on the 5th of September 2011. She is Fluent in English and French. She is married with one daughter.

ANTHONY JULIAN TAMBURRI is Dean of the John D. Calandra Italian American Institute (Queens College, CUNY). He holds a Ph.D. from the University of California, Berkeley. With Paolo Giordano and Fred Gardaphé, he is co-founder of Bordighera Press, past president of the Italian American Studies Association (then, American Italian Historical Association) and of the American Association of Teachers of Italian. He is also a member of numerous boards of directors, which include the Italian American Studies Association, IACE, ILICA, and the Italian Heritage and Culture Committee, NY. His authored books of the past decade include: *Semiotics of Re-reading: Guido Gozzano, Aldo Palazzeschi, and Italo Calvino* (2003); *Narrare altrove: diverse segnalature letterarie* (2007); *Una semiotica dell'etnicità: nuove segnalature per la letteratura italiano/americana* (2010); *Revisiting Italian Americana: Specificities and Generalities on Cinema* (2011); and *Re-reading Italian Americana: Specificities and Generalities on Literature and Criticism* (forthcoming). He is the executive producer of *Italics, The Italian American TV Magazine*, produced in collaboration with CUNY TV, and one of the co-founders of the Italian American Digital Project, parent organization of the portal i-Italy.org.

On November 17, 2011, then Ambassador GIULIO TERZI DI SANT'AGATA was sworn in by the President of the Republic as Minister for Foreign Affairs. This appointment by President of the Council of Ministers, Professor Mario Monti, is the latest in a long diplomatic career that has seen him directly engaged, both in Italy and abroad, in Italian foreign policy decisions concerning international security and the defence and promotion of national interests in the spheres of business, culture and research.

In his role as Ambassador of Italy to the United States, while engaged in the development of bilateral cooperation in the world's main crisis theatres, Giulio Terzi applied a strategy founded on the common cultural, human and economic values that constitute what Italy and the United States consider their "shared identity."

Transatlantic relations, international security, development and human rights concerns were the priority items on Giulio Terzi's agenda as Permanent Representative of Italy to the United Nations in New York from 2008 to 2009, where he led the Italian delegation to the Security Council in the final phase of Italy's 2007-2008 non-permanent membership – a period that placed Italy once again in the forefront in the campaign for Security Council reforms founded on the principles of efficiency, transparency and representation.

Other previous posts include that of Ambassador of Italy to Israel from 2002 to 2004, during which time, acting also as Italian EU Presidency representative, his focus was on strengthening the ties between Israel and Europe in an especially demanding context marked by the outbreak of the Second Intifada, a highly significant experience in which Giulio Terzi was able to gain a direct and even deeper understanding of Middle East issues. In the most recent phase of his tenure at the Foreign Ministry in Rome, Giulio Terzi fulfilled the functions of Deputy Secretary General, Director General for Multilateral Political Cooperation and Human Rights, and Political Director.

Born in Bergamo in 1946, Giulio Terzi completed a degree in Law, specialising in International Law, at the University of Milan.

INDEX

(Proper names and related associations and institutions)

Albert, Carl 51
Alighieri, Dante 5, 8, 23-24, 30, 73
American Association of Teachers of Italian (AATI) 54, 64, 68, 75
American Council on the Teaching of Foreign Languages (ACTFL) 1, 10, 11, 68, 69, 75
American Society for the Italian Legions of Merit (ASILM) 64
Aprile, Pino 69
Ardizzone, Tony 28
Armani, Giorgio 5

Baldacci, David 71
Barni, Monica 17
Barolini, Helen 25, 28
Barzini, Jr., Luigi 65-66
Bastianich, Lidia 33-34
Bisogniero, Claudio 73-76
Bloomberg, Michael R. 2
Boccaccio, Giovanni 73
Bolen, C. M. 51
Bonvino, Elisabetta 13
Bordage, Nicolas 12
Brambati, Massimo 43
Breward, Christopher 48
Burns, Max 51

Calabresi, Mario 17
Ciavolella, Massimo 17
Ciresi, Rita 71
Clinton, Bill 51
Coccia Foundation 67, 70
Coccia, Jr., Joseph 68
College Board 1, 5, 8, 39, 63, 64, 75
Columbus Citizens Foundation 64

Conference of Presidents of Major Italian American Organizations (COP) 63-64, 73
Cordova, Randy 12
Cucinelli, Brunello 49
Cuomo, Andrew 2

Dalla Montà, Lucia vi
Daniels, Roger 65
De Mauro, Tullio 17
Del Boca, Lorenzo 69
DeLillo, Don 71
Di Lauro, Rosa 51
DiPietro, Robert, 25-26
DiStasi, Lawrence 65
Dolci, Roberto 1-3, 51-61
Donato, Clorinda 8, 9-15
Dove, Rita 51
Doyle, D. 60

Easley Pearson, D. 52, 60
Eco, Umberto, 30
Escudé, Pierre 13, 14

Fellini, Federico 5
Fermi, Enrico 5
Filangieri, Gaetano 5, 7
Foderaro, Lisa 63
Fontana Sisters, 45
Fox, Steven R. 65
Franklin, Benjamin 5, 7
Friedman, Milton 51, 60
Furman, N. 17

Gambino, Christine 1
Gambino, Richard 27

83

Gardaphé, Fred 23-28
Gattinoni, Fernanda 45
Gattuso Hendin, Josephine 28
Gilbert, David 48
Gilbert, David 48
Gillespie, G. I. 52, 61
Giovanardi, C. 17
Goldberg, D. 17
Gregoriades, Cécile 12
Guarini, Frank 64

Haass, Richard, 69
Haller, Hermann 8, 17-21
Harvey, David 45
Hayward, F. M. 51, 52, 59

Inserra, Jr., Lawrence R. 68
Irving, John 51
Italian Consulate of New York 64
Italian Consulates 57
Italian Embassy in DC vi, 58, 64
Italian Heritage and Culture Committee of New York 64
Italian Language Foundation (ILF) 64
Italian Language Inter-Culture Alliance (ILICA) 68-70

Janin, Pierre 13
Jefferson, Thomas 75
Jimenez-Jimenez, A. 54, 60
John Agnew, 48
John D. Calandra Italian American Institute 1, 8, 57, 63, 71
Joseph and Elda Coccia Institute for the Italian Experience in America 67-68, 70

Kruze, L. 52, 60

La Scuola d'Italia Guglielmo Marconi 8, 75
Latour, Bruno 9, 15
Lusin, N. 17

Macchiarella, Gianclaudio 21
Maggipinto, Cristiano vi
Mangione, Jerre 26
Mangione, Silvana 29-31
Maraldi, Antonio 45
Marconi, Guglielmo 5
Marra, Vincenzo 35-37
Martin, Ricky 12
Mazzei, Filippo 75
McWhorter, John 69
Menghia, Catrinel 43
Meucci, Antonio 5
Michelli, Andrea 39-40
Middlebury College 75
Migliarotti, Gianluca 49
Milione, Vincenzo 1
Miraglia, L. 17
Mohajeri Norris, E. 52, 54
Montessori, Maria 6

Napolitano, Giorgio 73
National Italian American Foundation (NIAF) 57, 64, 75
National Organization of Italian American Women (NOIAW) 64
Northeast Conference on the Teaching of Foreign Languages (NECTFL) 68

Obama, Barack 75
Observatory of the Italian Language 58, 61, 75
Orahood, T. 52, 60
Order Sons of Italy in America (OSIA) 64

Ortoleva, Peppino 48

Paradiso, Berardo 39-41, 64
Pasolini, Pier Paolo 5
Pasquarelli-Gascon, Violetta 13
Pasternock, M. A. 54, 60
Paulicelli, Eugenia 43-49
Petrarca, Francesco 73
Plath, Sylvia 51
Puccini, Giacomo 41

Quintavalle, Natalia 7-8

Ramazzotti, Eros 12
Ricci, Matteo 35
Rice, Condoleezza 51
Rimanelli, Giose 28
Roosevelt, Theodore 51
Rossellini, Roberto 5
Rubin, D. L. 52
Rundstrom Williams, T. 55, 60
Rustin, Philana 12
Ryman J. 52, 60

Santosuosso J. J. 60
Saunders, Kay 65
Scottoline, Lisa 71
Severino, Roberto 21
Siaya L. M. 51, 52
Simone, Raffaelle 21
Spinelli, B. 55
Spolsky, B. 60
Steinberg, M. 59
Sutton, R. C. 52
Svevo, Italo 14

Tamburri, Anthony Julian 1-3, 63-71
Terzi di Sant'Agata, Giulio vi, 5-6, 64, 74
Thompson, J. W. 52

Tilman, M. 52
Trifone, P. 17
Trigiani, Adriana 71
Trooboff, S. 52, 60

UNESCO 34, 53, 74

University for Foreigners of Perugia 56, 57, 61, 64, 75, 76
Valentino 5
Van De Berg, M. 52, 60
Vedovelli, Massimo 17
Viscusi, Robert, 23-24

Watson, James 51
Wright, S. 60

Notes

Notes

www.ingramcontent.com/pod-product-compliance
Lightning Source LLC
Chambersburg PA
CBHW081642040426
42449CB00015B/3425